THE LONG FELLOW

THE
LONG FELLOW

*The Story of the Great Irish
Patriot, EAMON DE VALERA*

BY JACK STEFFAN

The Macmillan Company, New York

For Little Fitz,
and all her
lads and lassies

ACKNOWLEDGMENTS

MY DEEPEST GRATITUDE goes to all who have helped in the preparation of this book. Several I am not free to identify, but they have my heartfelt thanks, as do the following:

Barbara Lanigan, for suggesting the subject to me;

Julie Kernan, for her greatly appreciated introductions to friends in Dublin;

Julie McKone, who typed the manuscript so many times, for her patience and accuracy;

Nan Shields Karo, for her wise counsel in all things Irish;

The Hon. Thomas J. Kiernan, former Irish Ambassador to the United States, who very kindly smoothed the way for appointments in Dublin on my first visit there;

Patricia O'Mara Lavelle, for her kind hospitality and her generous permission to quote a paragraph from her biography of her father;

Alice Curtayne and Stephen Rynne, for their warm welcome and their books, which proved so enlightening;

My Franciscan friends, Fr. Cormac O'Daly, of Dublin, and Fr. Finbar Kenneally, of Washington, D.C., for their helpful suggestions and careful scrutiny of the manuscript;

Everyone at the Library of Congress, with especial gratitude to Legare H. B. Obear, Chief, Loan Division; and Edward N. MacConomy, Chief, Stack and Reader Division, for invaluable assistance in obtaining reference books and the granting of desk space where I might use them to best advantage;

Lois Watt, Chief, Educational Materials Laboratory, U.S. Office of Education, for the bountiful supply of biographies she so generously provided;

My perceptive and considerate editor, Dick Jackson, who not only helped me to untangle the intricacies of this complicated piece of Irish and American history, but also gave me unfailing encouragement during the long months it took to finish it;

And most of all, my sympathetic, Irish-loving husband, who warned me of all the difficulties I would encounter in writing about The Long Fellow, and then helped me in every way possible to surmount them.

God bless them all!

AUTHOR'S NOTE

MINDFUL OF the Irish saying "He who stays in the middle of the road deserves all the abuse that will be hurled at him from both sides," I decided about midway of this book that I must try to tell the de Valera story from what I felt was his viewpoint.

I came to my subject from the other side of the fence. My Scots-Irish father was born in Derry and my first taste of Irish history had a pronounced "Orange" flavor, while my mother's Irish ancestors were of the English Ascendancy persuasion. I think, therefore, it may be fairly said that after a careful examination of all the available evidence, I chose to be pro-de Valera out of honest conviction.

We are told over and again that he is a controversial figure, but so was our Abraham Lincoln, and, for that matter, every strong President we have had in the United States. May all who read this book go on to read as many more Irish and English histories and biographies as they can lay their hands on, and then make up their own minds about Ireland's "Dev."

JACK STEFFAN

CONTENTS

President of Ireland EAMON DE VALERA with John
Fitzgerald Kennedy in Dublin, June 1963

"Ireland's role is unique, for every new nation knows
that Ireland was the first of the small nations of the
Twentieth Century to win its struggle for independence."
President John F. Kennedy—
Speech to the Irish Parliament—
June 28, 1963

PROLOGUE

THIS IS THE unlikely story of an unusual man, of his incredible rise to power, of his successful campaign against impossible odds to win freedom for his country. And because such a crusade is never waged alone, it is also the story of Irish patriots who fought beside Eamon de Valera and in some cases against him—but always, they believed, for the good of Ireland.

THE IRISH

PATRICK PEARSE
(*Executed by the British, 1916*)

PROF. EOIN MacNEILL

JOHN REDMOND

SIR ROGER CASEMENT
(*Executed by the British, 1916*)

CATHAL BRUGHA
(Killed in action—Irish civil war, 1922)

ARTHUR GRIFFITH, left, with
Eamon de Valera

MICHAEL COLLINS, right, with Arthur Griffith (*Collins killed in action—Irish civil war, 1922*)

COUNT PLUNKETT

AUSTIN STACK

RICHARD MULCAHY

ERSKINE CHILDERS
(*Executed by Irish Free State
Government, 1922*)

HARRY BOLAND, left, with
Michael Collins (*Boland shot by an
Irish Free State soldier, 1922*)

WILLIAM COSGRAVE

KEVIN O'HIGGINS
(*Assassinated, 1927*)

EAMON DE VALERA watching St. Patrick's Day parade in New York City

GAVAN DUFFY

EAMON DUGGAN, right,
with Eoin MacNeill

DR. DOUGLAS HYDE

PRESIDENT and MRS. DE VALERA

THE BRITISH

RT. HON.
WINSTON CHURCHILL

PRIME MINISTER LLOYD GEORGE

RT. HON. BONAR LAW

SIR JAMES CRAIG
(LORD CRAIGAVON)
left, and SIR EDWARD
CARSON

LORD FRENCH

LORD BIRKENHEAD

SIR HENRY WILSON

RT. HON.
AUSTEN CHAMBERLAIN

"A dream! a dream! an ancient dream!
  Yet ere peace come to Innisfail,
  Some weapons on some field must gleam,
  Some burning glory fire the Gael."
    "Ways of War"—*Lionel Johnson*

1

COMMANDANT

OF THE THIRD

DUBLIN, IRELAND, never saw a more beautiful morning, nor one that looked more peaceful than the late-April Easter Monday of the year 1916.

Gray sodden clouds that had hung low above the city through a long winter were shredded white by a lively breeze, and the sky beyond was a brilliant blue. It was a perfect day for a brisk walk in the country. And there were some brisk walkers on the streets of Dublin.

"Who's the Long Fellow?" piped a childish voice from a white-curtained window as a handful of armed men swung past. At their head was a tall commandant in a gray-green uniform, his mouth set firmly below a brown mustache, brown eyes staring straight ahead as he marched.

"Ah, what difference does it make who he is?" scoffed the child's nurse, then, raising her voice, "Them's the Irish Volunteers, playing soldier. If they want to fight, why don't they go fight the Germans with the rest of our boys?"

The taunt carried clearly to the ears of Commandant de Valera, but he paid no more attention to it than to the cries of the gulls hurrying eastward to swoop and soar in a freshening wind above the glittering blue waters of the Irish Sea.

True, more than a hundred fifty thousand Irish soldiers were fighting and dying for England in the muddy trenches of World War I. After more than seven hundred years of English rule, most of Ireland had come to bear the English yoke with resignation. But now, as in every generation for the last seven hundred years, there were Irish patriots who chose instead to fight for Irish freedom. The Volunteers were not playing soldier this morning. There were real bullets in their odd assortment of firearms.

The burden of stationing his depleted forces where they could best use those bullets sent Eamon de Valera's long legs into an even longer stride and the men following had to double-time to keep pace with him. As they hurried along they listened, straining their ears for the sound of guns. When would the first shot be fired? And where? Were the Volunteers rising outside Dublin, or had their leaders' conflicting orders thrown everyone into confusion?

Ireland's Easter Rising had been well planned. For more than seven hundred years the coldly realistic motto of the Irish patriot had been *England's extremity is Ireland's opportunity!* Only when, as now, England was embroiled elsewhere in war did an Irish rebellion have the slightest chance for success.

And this rising had the additional advantage of help from sympathizers in the United States, where men of the secret I.R.B., the Irish Republican Brotherhood, had ordered and paid for a whole shipload of arms and ammunition which the Germans were to deliver on the west coast of Ireland during Holy Week. If that shipment had been safely landed; if every Volunteer had clockworked into position at the appointed time that Sunday morning, the Rising might well have been the decisive and final battle in Ireland's long struggle to be free.

Almost better not to hope for freedom than to see such a noble plan fail. But in the last few days officers of the Volunteers had disagreed—violently. And yesterday a notice published by their commander-in-chief prohibited all Easter Sunday maneuvers whatsoever. That notice cut in half the forces who had reported today, Monday. Worse, it practically canceled in the outlying towns the action that had been masterfully designed to disperse the British forces and give the Dublin Brigade time to secure the capital. It was enough to make St. Patrick stop praying for Ireland entirely. . . .

But if such a thing were possible, the English were even more confused than the Volunteers. For months British Intelligence in both Dublin and the United States had been submitting reports of an Irish rebellion in the making. Ridiculing the notion, the British Chief Secretary had gone off to London for a long holiday weekend. That Easter Monday saw most of the English officers of the Dublin garrison go trooping out of the city to the Fairytown Races. And although three British officials had been sitting in troubled conference since early morning behind the gray walls of Dublin Castle, they were heartened by the fortunate events of the past weekend.

Early on Good Friday, one of His Majesty's patrol boats off the southwest coast of Ireland had overhauled a suspicious-looking vessel and was taking her into port when suddenly the crew took to the lifeboats, broke out a German flag, and blew up the vessel. Shortly afterward a man hiding on the shore was discovered to be that Irish patriot and traitor to England Sir Roger Casement, just arrived from Germany. It was a relief to the British to have *him* safely behind bars in a London prison.

The bad luck of the Irish hotheads had apparently brought

them to a more temperate point of view. On the table before the Assistant Secretary in Dublin Castle was yesterday's *Irish Independent,* a small notice marked off in red:

Owing to the very critical position, all orders given to Irish Volunteers for Easter Sunday are hereby rescinded and no parades, marches or other movements of Irish Volunteers will take place.

The order was signed by Professor Eoin MacNeill, head of the well-drilled, highly disciplined, the devil-knew-how-well-armed and—British officials were convinced—*seditious* military organization that numbered in the thousands and was spread all over Ireland. MacNeill's name was high on the list of rebel leaders scheduled for arrest in the next day or so.

But, as the Assistant Secretary bent over a letter to his chief, he congratulated himself that the immediate danger was over. Thanks to English good fortune and Professor Mac-Neill, Easter Sunday had passed without incident. Surely, as in every Irish revolt, Divine Providence was on the side of the English.

It came as a greater shock, therefore, when that first shot for which Eamon de Valera's Third Battalion had been listening went off a few minutes before noon on Monday at the very gates of Dublin Castle. The Volunteers could not know how small was the force inside, so, in the first few moments of the rebellion, they hesitated. A quick-witted guard slammed the gates. The opportunity was lost.

It was but one more link in the chain of misfortune that stretched back to the flare-up among their officers, the capture of Casement, the loss of the shipload of arms and ammunition. The devil's own luck had dogged them.

No wonder Eoin MacNeill had tried to stop the Rising. He had always maintained that the Volunteers should fight only in self-defense. The whole rebellion had been planned without his knowledge, the other officers hoping once the troops went into action, MacNeill would come around. Discovering their plans ahead of time, he exploded in rage. And any thought of his agreeing to them was blasted by news of the disasters. But no matter how sound MacNeill's reasoning, there were men of the Volunteers, of Labor's Citizen Army, of the secret I.R.B. who believed they must strike for freedom now or see their country forever enslaved.

As the shot rang out at the gates of Dublin Castle, a new tricolor of orange, white, and green was unfurled above the General Post Office and from its steps the poet and scholar Patrick Pearse proclaimed to a group of startled bystanders the formation of a new Provisional Government and the independence of Ireland.

To the southeast, across the river Liffey, the tall young de Valera ordered the remnants of his Third Battalion toward Westland Row Station and Boland's Mill. He needed four times the number of men who had reported that morning to defend this vitally important area.

"As soon as they get the news in London," Pearse had said to him, "they will send reinforcements. It is your job to hold them off as long as possible. . . ."

The main port serving Dublin was Kingstown, six miles or so to the south and east. British forces landing there would come by train into Westland Row Station, or march along the main road which paralleled the railway and bridged the Grand Canal at Lower Mount Street.

From a military point of view, Dublin was an island, bisected by the deep, smooth, brown-flowing Liffey, encircled by the waterways and locks of the Grand Canal. Few Dublin streets did not, eventually, have to take to a bridge.

De Valera sent men into the three-story stucco Clanwilliam House overlooking Lower Mount Street, and posted a few crack shots in buildings along the road leading to the bridge. To keep the English troops bottled up in Beggars Bush Barracks, one of his enterprising Volunteers broke through the back wall and into a shop right across the street from the main gate.

A small detachment dashed into Westland Row Station to cut telephone wires and clear out an angry holiday-bound crowd who couldn't believe the soldiers were in earnest. One Volunteer finally had to aim his rifle at a trainload of incredulous travelers and send two companions forward with drawn bayonets before he could persuade passengers to leave the train and the station. Once the place was cleared, Volunteers seized signal boxes and barricaded doors with overturned seats and slot machines.

The Catholics among them scarcely knew what to do when two priests came over a barricade.

"We're acting under orders from our commandant," said one soldier stubbornly, but he went to his knees when the priest replied simply, "Then we'll hear your confessions."

Outside the station a Volunteer ran along the top of the railway embankment, prying up rails, battering switches, and shouting to a lingering crowd at the foot of the embankment that Ireland was free and they had a new Republic. They jeered at him until shots from a sniper on a distant rooftop sent them diving for cover like quail into a hedge.

Eamon de Valera set up his Third Battalion headquarters in Boland's Bakery and behind the smoke-grimed walls of Boland's Mill, which bordered the canal. He ordered a breach in the back wall of the bakery and a ramp built up to the railway line. Now his long legs could take him quickly throughout the area and he was constantly on the move.

By afternoon they could hear firing from all over the city. An English officer on his way back to Beggars Bush Barracks was killed when he tried to interfere with Volunteers barricading Clanwilliam Place. Except for that, nearby streets were quiet.

Streetcars had stopped running everywhere in Dublin. Few

vehicles of any kind ventured out. At St. Stephen's Green, not many blocks away, the Volunteers were digging in and their outposts commandeered every car that came along and made its driver run it into a barricade. It was from that direction the men at Boland's Bakery could hear the most constant peppering of shots.

Concerned about the possibility of fires resulting from broken gas mains, de Valera ordered the adjacent gasworks seized and partially dismantled. Since much of Dublin was lighted by gas, this action blacked out a large part of the city as well as cut the power supply and shut off gas burners on all the stoves.

That night as the commandant prowled restlessly inside Boland's Mill he came suddenly on a group of sentries kneeling in a half circle, murmuring their rosaries.

"Get to your posts!" he ordered.

Tonight each man would have to do his praying by himself. But he could not be harsh with them. Some were no more than boys. One looked so young de Valera had sent him home three times that day, but he kept popping up and at last was allowed to stay.

At the bakery a messenger awaited him with news from other parts of the city. Volunteers at the Post Office had fired on a company of British Lancers, killed three riders and a number of horses.

The poor of Dublin—very poor indeed that year of 1916— had taken advantage of the rebellion to break windows and make off with everything they could carry.

Patrick Pearse had foreseen something of the kind and had warned against it in his proclamation:

We place the cause of the Irish Republic under the protection of the Most High God, whose blessing we invoke upon our arms, and we pray that no one who serves that cause will dishonor it by cowardice, inhumanity or rapine. . . .

Few among the unruly crowds had even stopped to read his words.

As the night deepened, the wildest rumors flashed across the embattled city:

"All Ireland is rising!"

"Thousands of Irish-Americans are landing in the west."

"There is a German fleet offshore, a German submarine in the bay!"

De Valera shook his head at that last one. He and the rest of the Volunteers would welcome a German invasion no more than they did the English troops that occupied Ireland. Across the face of Liberty Hall, where many Volunteers had assembled that morning, a banner blazoned: WE SERVE NEITHER KING NOR KAISER, BUT IRELAND!

But de Valera encouraged the spreading of the stories. The outnumbered Volunteers had to use any weapon handy, and these rumors were good psychological warfare. He even manufactured a few yarns of his own, recklessly multiplying the forces of the Third Battalion and magnifying the amount of their military equipment until they sounded able to defend the whole city by themselves.

He was too good a mathematician to be deluded by his own stories or those told by anyone else. The only thing that could save the Rising was more men. Fighting men. If the people of Dublin would only respond to the eloquent plea of Pearse's proclamation:

IRISHMEN and IRISHWOMEN: In the Name of God and of the dead generations from which she receives her old tradition of nationhood, Ireland, through us, summons her children to her flag and strikes for her freedom. . . .

How Eamon de Valera had thrilled to this Irish Declaration of Independence! The dream of Irish freedom had been a fire to warm his heart by since the long-ago day a teacher of the Christian Brothers told him of Sarsfield and O'Neill, and Red Hugh O'Donnell, who fled from Ireland to Spain. His father, Vivion de Valera, had come from Spain. Eamon's brown eyes, his light brown hair and sallow skin were his Spanish inheritance. To some they made him look strangely un-Irish, but his more than six feet of height, broad shoulders, the high dreamer's forehead, and big robust body were like his mother's brothers', the Colls of County Limerick. And he may have had from them too the fiery temper he found so hard to control. Nothing made it flare more quickly than the suggestion that he was something less than Irish.

But what did those watching, indifferent crowds of Easter Monday care about their country? How little they knew of Ireland! They had been educated in schools whose courses of study were so controlled no mention was ever made of Irish greatness. They read only newspapers edited by British propagandists, voted for representatives who sat in a British Parliament—why, even their police force was commanded by the British. And Ireland was occupied by British soldiers, while her own were off fighting a British war. Those who jeered loudest at the Volunteers were always the "Separation Women," who drew regular compensation checks because their men were in the British Army.

For de Valera, that Monday night seemed to last forever. When Tuesday dawned at last it was gray and dark, with rain sluicing down the gutters. From across the Liffey came the constant rattle of gunfire. By noon it was punctuated by the thudding jar of artillery.

Taking stock of their position in the misty light, the commandant decided he had neglected a most strategic post, the empty distillery building close by. If the British should occupy it, they could bring both mill and bakery under fire from above. And if they believed the rebels were inside, the British might waste a good bit of valuable ammunition on the tall building.

He brought out a green flag decorated with a golden harp. The tricolor might be the flag of the Rising, but to most people the green flag still meant Ireland, and he ordered this one flown above the distillery. During the afternoon he sent a Volunteer to wigwag signals from the distillery roof and that night lights shone from some of its windows. The ruse was a complete success. Two days later the New York *Times* printed what their reporter thought he had witnessed:

The distillery was the scene of one of the sharpest little battles of the uprising. The rebels were forced out of the flour mill by bombardment and many of them were seen, covered with flour, making their way to the distillery. Once there they hoisted the rebel flag, which floated from the corner of a square tower. . . .

The account was as accurate as any of the others that slipped through the net of censorship imposed by the British. In Dublin on Tuesday there were two published reports of the fighting; they could not have been more contradictory.

"The authorities have taken active and energetic measures to cope with the situation," said the pro-British *Irish Times,* while Patrick Pearse's official communiqué gave a glowing report of how the Volunteers were holding all their positions with the British forces nowhere able to break through. His boast that Volunteers were rising all over Ireland was without foundation. But inside the capital they had dug themselves into half a dozen well-fortified positions and were bluffing the fortification of many more.

Wednesday dawned clear and warm. De Valera's scouts reported no movement of troops along the approaches to the city which they guarded. Whatever English soldiers had been in Beggars Bush Barracks were still there.

During the morning a British gunboat moved up the river Liffey and began to lob shells toward Liberty Hall, where the Volunteers had assembled two days before and which, according to British Intelligence, still held hundreds of rebel soldiers. The British gunner's aim was poor, but no worse than the false information from his intelligence service. The only person in the building was the caretaker, who broke all records for the hundred-yard dash across the street when the first shell landed nearby.

Not a single Irish rebel was hit, although the bombardment continued until only the walls were standing, the building next door was in ruins, and some unwary civilians were wounded on the street. Then the gunboat dropped back down river and took aim on the distillery.

At the same time a British field gun began to fire blindly in that direction. The watching Third Battalion cheered as the first shell sent a fountain of water blossoming over gunboat and crew.

"What rotten shots!" cried Commandant de Valera gleefully, as a second shell splashed into the river.

It was a hit-or-miss bombardment. At last one shell from the gunboat pierced a tank on the distillery roof and sent water cascading down the walls, but when night fell the green flag was still flying; the distillery walls still stood. Best of all, scarcely a shell had fallen near the bakery.

But the English reinforcements had landed at Kingstown that morning. Warned to take less-traveled routes into the city, they thought the warnings were a trick. A third of the detachment marched toward Dublin along the road toward Mount Street Bridge and into the crossfire of de Valera's outposts.

It was later estimated that eight hundred British soldiers came that afternoon along the main route from Kingstown. Houses garrisoned by the Third Battalion held only thirteen men, but they poured bullets into the marching column that sent the English reeling back, leaving dead and wounded soldiers strewn all over road and bridge.

The other two-thirds of the British reinforcements reached

the heart of Dublin in safety along different routes, but British officers of this detachment continued to send wave after wave of soldiers against the superbly defended Mount Street Bridge. For five hours with rifles, machine guns and grenades, they continued the attack. Rebel-held Clanwilliam House went up in flames. Seven of the thirteen defenders were dead, the rest escaped or captured, but the British dared not cross the bridge that night. They picked up their own casualties—two hundred thirty-four of them, half the British losses in the entire Rising—and waited for morning.

The Dublin air reeked with smoke, the sky glowed red with flames from burning O'Connell Street, fires set by British field guns at Trinity College and the gunboat in the Liffey, from machine guns on top of the Customs House and the Fire Station Tower.

At Boland's Mill Eamon de Valera moved from one command post to another, at times showing such a reckless disregard for danger that his men tried to hold him back. Once he watched a Volunteer with a rifle trying to silence a British sniper on a nearby roof.

"Let me have that gun," de Valera said suddenly, stepped out into the open, took aim, fired—and his men saw the sniper fall.

"You shouldn't take such chances," protested an aide.

The commandant shrugged aside his restraining hand. "Better men than I have been killed."

"That may be so," said the loyal aide, "but the way the men feel, if you got hit, in ten minutes there wouldn't be any more Third Battalion."

"Not my men," said Eamon de Valera. He had more faith in them than that.

He had not slept. He could not have said how long it was since he had slept. On the night of Holy Thursday, in the little house within earshot of these guns, he had said goodbye to his wife and looked at his four small sleeping children.

Whatever rest he had had since then was in short snatches from which he must rouse to instant alertness, ready to give a necessary order, to march, to attack, to do whatever was required of him.

De Valera was not a soldier by profession, but a teacher of mathematics. He cared nothing for politics. Love for Ireland had taken him into the Volunteers. As clearly as MacNeill himself, he had foreseen the failure of the Rising. But on the warm, sunny Thursday morning after Easter, even with the struggle turning against them, with British snipers moving ever closer across the rooftops, with fire eating into the heart of Dublin and clouds of acrid, pungent smoke rolling skyward, de Valera would not have changed places with anyone in the world. His Third Battalion had accomplished miracles. They were defending their area so successfully the British thought it held a hundred times their number.

Some of the smaller garrisons in other parts of the city were not so fortunate. By Thursday afternoon, one after another began to give up. From the General Post Office came news that a commanding officer of the Volunteers was severely wounded. And the next day, Friday, April 28, Patrick Pearse's communiqué was a prelude to a wholesale surrender.

If the men who fought do not win this fight, they will at least have deserved to win it . . . they have redeemed Dublin from many shames, and made her name splendid among the names of cities.

O'Connell Street was in ruins and now the flames were eating into the Post Office itself. The wounded officer was carried to safety on a stretcher. Another Volunteer leader was killed as he dashed across the street. The Post Office was evacuated at the cost of seventeen casualties.

Civilians—men, women, even children—were being killed in the streets. Everyone was hungry. There was no meat, no bread, no milk. Since Tuesday the skies had been clear. Unseasonable heat parched throats and made the rooftops almost unbearable for snipers, Volunteers and British alike.

On Saturday Pearse knew he could fight no longer. At nine o'clock that night, he and the main body of Volunteers marched to the Parnell Monument and stacked their arms.

Men of the Third Battalion could not believe the news. It was late Sunday afternoon before a courier from Pearse could persuade Commandant de Valera that he must surrender also. Some of his men smashed their guns on the pavement rather than let the British have them. What a magnificent lot they were! To the English officer who arrived to take charge, de Valera said, "Shoot me if you want to, but take care of my men!"

He handed over his rifle, his field glasses, and marched away hatless, brown hair unkempt, mustache bedraggled, his long legs wrapped in untidy leggings, uniform drab with flour dust and dirt. Most of the crowd that gathered watched in silence, but at one muffled jeer, de Valera's bloodshot eyes burned and anger rose in him like a tide.

"Ah," he said bitterly, "if the people had only come out with knives and forks!"

"Life springs from death; and from the graves of
patriot men and women spring living nations."
Patrick Pearse

2

AN END AND
A BEGINNING

By SUNDAY EVENING, April 30, 1916, the Dublin prisons could
not hold all those who had been arrested. Commandant de
Valera was taken to a fire station and locked in a small room
next to the engine.

He stared about him, scarcely realizing where he was, or
that the long strain was ended. It was like a dream when
someone spoke to him from a window.

"We're going out on an alarm," said a fireman's harsh
whisper. "Come through here and jump on—we'll have you
away fast enough."

The man disappeared. Eamon de Valera started toward
the window, stopped. If he escaped, what would happen to
his men? He heard the fire signal. Beyond that window was
freedom—but as engine and crew clattered off, Commandant
de Valera turned back and sat down to wait for whatever
might happen.

He slept fitfully, woke, and slept again, too drugged with

fatigue to think clearly, yet seeing with singular vividness his home, his beautiful wife, his children. He had known as he strode away from them that night of Holy Thursday how slim the chance he would ever see them again. But there were times in a man's life when he must choose something greater than his own happiness, greater even than the welfare of those he loved.

What a strange circumstance had brought Eamon de Valera here! He was of Irish descent but not of Irish birth. Catherine Coll, the young girl who was to become his mother, left Ireland in the tragic famine year of 1879. They called it the year when the crowbar went under the doorsill, for British landlords were not satisfied merely to evict those who could not pay their rent. The walls of their cabins were leveled, and many a desperate Irish family had to shelter themselves in a ditch.

The Colls of Bruree were by no means in such dreadful straits, but there were few opportunities in Ireland for the ambitious, attractive young Catherine and she went off to America where a brother, Edmund, had already settled himself.

In New York Catherine met and married a young Spanish musician, Vivion de Valera. They made a home for themselves in Manhattan near Forty-third Street and Lexington Avenue, where, a year from the following October, Eamon was born. He was christened, his grandmother liked to remind him, across the street in the fine Catholic Church of St. Agnes.

Eamon could not remember much of those early years. He was often told that it was a happy home, full of music and stories of great Spanish and Irish heroes. Perhaps to increase his pride in his father's people, it was also his grandmother's fancy to repeat often the prophecy of one of Ireland's great saints that Ireland's salvation would come from Spain.

The flame of Irish patriotism was alight in the small

Eamon before he was three years old, as a friendly English neighbor discovered one day when he tried to persuade the boy to wave a British flag and instead saw it dashed to the sidewalk.

Not long after that Eamon's father was on his way to the Rocky Mountains. A doctor, discovering that he had tuberculosis, thought he might find a cure in the high, dry air of Colorado. But the disease was too far advanced. Vivion de Valera died there and his grieving widow, left with a three-year-old son and little money, knew she would again have to go to work.

There was no one to care for the boy. When Edmund Coll stopped for a visit on his way to Ireland, where he hoped to recover from the malaria that had plagued him in upper New York State, Catherine sadly put small Eamon in his arms and sent him off to her mother and another brother, Patrick, in Bruree.

Greatly as Catherine de Valera loved her native Ireland, it was still a most distressful country. "When I am able," she vowed, "I will go and fetch him." What chance would her son have there?

But after the long voyage, as the bright green hills of their homeland came into sight over the heaving waters, the homesick Irish lined the rail of the little ship and Eamon heard his uncle Edmund singing with the rest:

> *Oh, Ireland, isn't it grand you look,*
> *Like a bride in her rich adorning,*
> *With all the pent-up love of my heart*
> *I bid you the top of the morning!*

And it was a warm family welcome the two of them got in the little house beside the country road that meandered off to Bruree. Edmund stretched his visit as long as he could and grew strong and hearty again in the clean fresh air of County

Limerick, nourished by the good plain food that Eamon's grandmother knew so well how to prepare.

Eamon grew like one of the willows that shot up along the marshy borders of the river Maigue. With a true Irish reverence for learning, his Uncle Patrick put him in school at age five and the boy dived into his letters as a salmon fingerling swims eagerly through tidewater to the freedom of the ocean.

A farm boy has to put his back into the work, but there was time to play, time to explore the ancient castle ruins that thrust their broken walls and towers from the distant green-hedged fields. And there was time to linger on the old stone bridge that arched across the river at Bruree and listen to tales of the wars that had destroyed those castles.

Bruree was a village set down in the wide valley of the Maigue, its misty blue sky always freighted with great gray clouds sailing in from the Atlantic. Some of the land in County Limerick was thin and poorly drained, but the grass was a lush bright green, and his Uncle Patrick's cows produced plenty of rich milk that had to be taken to the creamery. It was a poky job, but the boy took advantage of the long waiting in line with his donkey cart. As he waited he read stories of heroes and high adventure.

In this westerly county of Limerick, with its neighbor County Clare to the north across the river Shannon, the Irish had held out longest against conquering English armies. In the city of Limerick not twenty miles away was the great stone where Patrick Sarsfield had signed a treaty with the English three hundred years before. It was an honorable treaty, wrung from the English military leaders by Sarsfield's masterful command of the Irish armies, and by the people of Limerick itself, where every man, woman, and child had joined in a bloody battle against the invaders.

I call to your mind brave Sarsfield,
And the battle in Limerick Street,

The mine and the shattered wall,
And the battered breach held good,
And the English in full retreat. . . .

So went the ballad an old neighbor used to sing. But one of the books in the Coll home was the *Life of Patrick Sarsfield,* and from it Eamon learned the sad tale of how that treaty, signed by the British military, was broken by British politicians. Rather than live under alien rule, Sarsfield left his homeland forever and was followed into exile by thousands of Ireland's bravest soldiers.

Later Eamon heard many a tale of the Penal Days that followed, when an Irishman no longer dared to speak the name of his country. Speak of her the Irish did, of course, and all the more because she was so oppressed, writing poems to her as if she were a sweetheart, with never a mention of Ireland, but calling her instead Dark Rosaleen, or Cathleen ni Houlihan, or the Poor Old Woman.

As the oppression worsened, not only was a man forbidden to love Ireland, but even his religion was forbidden him. One after another the Penal Laws deprived Catholics of their rights until the covetous British were enabled to seize their good Irish land, until a Catholic was no longer allowed to educate his children, until he might not even own a fine horse if a Protestant chose to offer for it the mean sum of five English pounds.

Catholic priests with a bounty on their heads were hunted like wolves. Catholic bishops were imprisoned and tortured, at least one of them hanged, drawn and quartered, and his severed head impaled on an iron stake. Catholic churches were desecrated—late in the nineteenth century Eamon found such things hard to believe, yet there was evidence of that last outrage in this very house, for had not a priest long ago brought to his grandmother a consecrated altar stone from the ruins of a church? On one occasion when she was ill, had not another priest come and said Mass there . . . ?

A welcome guest of the Colls was an old man who spoke Gaelic, the ancient Irish language. Eamon's grandmother could speak it too, and the boy picked up many words and phrases as he listened, although the old storyteller spoke so fast it was impossible to understand all he said. His were wonderful tales of great Irish saints, of Irish kings and fighting men and poets, of the days when Christian Ireland was sending missionaries to the barbarians of Europe and England.

It was not only listening to stories and reading books that Eamon loved, however. He also loved mathematics. He became such an eager and inquiring student that the old schoolmaster advised Patrick to put him under the care of the Christian Brothers at Rathluirc. Their school was six miles away and it demanded quite a sacrifice from his uncle to send the boy there, but he managed it somehow.

Eamon and a companion went each morning by train to Rathluirc. The afternoon train ran so late they seldom waited for it, preferring to walk or run the six miles home. Eamon enjoyed sports and on this daily trek he sprinted as fast as he could over varying distances and presently was able to outrun most of the boys in Bruree. It was probably about that time he decided he would never smoke or drink. The temperance movement in Ireland had spread over Ireland from the time of Father Mathew's great campaign in the first half of the nineteenth century, and the people of Bruree (especially the women) were strongly in favor of it, but Eamon's decision was tied up more closely with his desire to excel in athletics.

A game of hurley in a field alongside the road was bound to delay his homeward journey. Bruree had a champion hurley team and Eamon delighted in the rough-and-tumble of this Irish form of hockey.

He grew so fast it was hard to keep him in clothes. He was almost as tall as the six-foot-four-inch Patrick at sixteen, when he won a scholarship to Blackrock College in County Dublin. There his athletic ability and his quiet, self-confident manner soon made a place for him among other students, while his genuine love of learning made his professors prophesy for him all kinds of scholastic honors.

He was out of school, himself a teacher, when in 1907 his mother came from New York for a visit. True to her vow, she had come to take him back to America. He loved her with the deep devotion most Irishmen cherish for their mothers, but he refused to go with her. She did not really need him. She had remarried. There were two other children. And the deepest ties of Eamon de Valera's heart bound him to Ireland.

So his mother sailed for New York without him, her disappointment tempered by pride. Eamon missed her, but he kept busy with his teaching and, outside school hours, he spent a good deal of time studying Gaelic. The Gaelic League was trying to revive the language and Eamon had enrolled in one of its classes. His instructor was a beautiful girl with a mass of red-gold hair. Her name was Janet Flanagan, in English—but she chose to be known by her Irish name, Sinead, which she pronounced Shin-*nee*.

In 1910 Sinead and Eamon de Valera were married. By then he was teaching his favorite subject, mathematics, and they settled down to the quiet, scholarly life both of them enjoyed. The next five years were hopeful ones, the happiest Eamon had ever known. A son, Vivion, was born, then a daughter, Maureen. In another year Eamon, Jr., arrived, and in 1915, Brian.

During those five years the Irish political pot came to a frothing boil. The English Parliament passed a bill enabling Irish farmers to buy the land which had for centuries been owned by English landlords. Another bill was introduced promising Home Rule for Ireland. But in Northeast Ulster, especially around Belfast, families of British descent, the political and financial leaders of the area, swore that if Home Rule were forced on them they would fight.

Members of the party that was out of power in England encouraged their rebellion. After all, if they stirred up enough trouble, the government party might have to resign and its opponents could be elected. With a callous disregard for everything but their own political advantage, Sir Edward Carson, Bonar Law, and Captain James Craig egged on the anti-Home Rule and bitterly anti-Catholic "Orange" forces in the North. They bought a shipment of guns from Germany, and armed men began to drill openly in Belfast. When the Prime Minister sent young Winston Churchill to Belfast to speak for Home Rule, he was not permitted to enter Ulster Hall and had to hold his meeting in a football field.

"Whatever Ulster's right may be, she cannot stand in the way of the whole of Ireland," protested Churchill. Besides, not all Ulster was in revolt. "Half-a-province," Churchill called it, and declared that they could not "obstruct forever a reconciliation between the British and Irish democracies!"

But when English officers at The Curragh, an army camp not far from Dublin, were directed to go to Belfast and restore order, they refused, saying they would resign their commissions first.

It was perhaps a teapot tempest, but it was taken seriously by the German Kaiser. In the confident belief that threat of civil war in Ulster would keep England from coming to Belgium's aid, the Kaiser planned to send his armies into that small country and launch the first great world war.

In response to the challenge from Belfast, the Irish Volunteers were organized in Dublin. One of the first to join was Eamon de Valera. A natural leader, he was soon made an officer. In 1914, when the Volunteers received their first shipment of arms, he commanded one of the companies that marched to Howth to receive them.

That was a day to try the temper of any organization. Except for a few officers, the Volunteers had no idea that this was not just another routine, boring march. When the white yacht of the Anglo-Irish Erskine Childers suddenly sailed out from behind a small island and came alongside the quay, they stared in puzzled surprise. But as the first box came ashore and was broken open—when they saw the guns— they broke ranks and pushed forward in an undisciplined rush that almost forced those in front into the water.

One of the few officers to hold his company in place, Eamon de Valera was as eager as any to get his own rifle in his hands, and he would never forget the feel of the weapon as he shouldered it to march away. He sympathized with those he saw who carefully put their own guns under a guarding boot before passing weapons on to their fellows.

The English had made no move to stop the Ulstermen from arming themselves. In Dublin, however, when news came of the landing at Howth, a company of British soldiers marched off to intercept the returning Volunteers and seize their guns. They captured only a few, for while Volunteer officers parleyed with the English commander, the Irish soldiers vanished over hedges, through gardens, down side streets, scattering like rabbits in a hayfield.

During the afternoon a strolling crowd in Bachelor's Walk jeered at the British detachment for its failure to disarm the Volunteers. The infuriated soldiers fired into the crowd, killed three civilians (one of them a woman) and wounded many more. Clearly there was one law for the militant half of Ulster, quite another for all the rest of Ireland.

That was July 26, 1914. A little over a week later, England declared war on Germany. And John Redmond, head of the Irish delegation in the British Parliament, pledged first that the Irish Volunteers would defend their country against invasion, then proceeded to tell them it would be a disgrace if they did not join England in the fighting.

"Ireland has no blood to give to any land, to any cause, but that of Ireland," protested Sir Roger Casement.

"Ireland is not at war with Germany," wrote Arthur Griffith in his paper, *Sinn Fein* (pronounced Shin Fane, the Gaelic for "Ourselves Alone"). "We are Irish Nationalists and the only duty we can have is to stand for Ireland's interests."

The Irish Volunteers split, most of their hundred eighty thousand going with Redmond. Eamon de Valera was one of the eight to ten thousand who refused.

Three weeks after England entered the war, members of the secret I.R.B. began to plan how to use that small but dedicated group in an insurrection. It was two years before they could launch their Rising, and during those years all of England's effective wartime propaganda was turned against any Irishman who refused to enlist in the British army. He was called pro-German, a slacker, yellow. . . .

Now the Rising was over. It had failed. But whatever people might call the Volunteers who had fought so valiantly, it would not be cowards.

"I suppose Dublin is blaming us for bringing martial law upon the city," thought Eamon de Valera. General Sir John Maxwell had been put in complete charge of the city. By the time he arrived from London, the revolt was practically over, but he swore to round up every rebel in Ireland and give him rough justice.

"They say Maxwell has had a grave dug big enough to hold a hundred and fifty of us," said a companion the day de Valera was moved to a chill, unfurnished room in crowded Richmond Barracks.

Each prisoner had received, in writing, the charge against him: *Rebellion, with the intent of assisting the enemy.* No one had to be told that in wartime such a charge meant death.

Commandant de Valera heard bits and pieces of the court-martial proceedings that began Tuesday morning, May 2. Patrick Pearse, first to appear, faced three officers of the court, the prosecutor, and witnesses for the prosecution. He was allowed no counsel to plead for him; no witnesses could be called in his defense. Each prisoner, they told him, would be allowed to make a statement. Pearse made his proudly. For the past week he had done as charged—commanded the forces of the Irish Republic.

"When I was a child of ten," said Patrick Pearse, "I went down on my knees one night and promised God that I should devote my life to an effort to free my country. I have kept that promise."

But he had *not* aided England's enemy. The Volunteers had been sent only German arms. They had neither asked for nor accepted German money or military help.

"My aim was to win Irish freedom," declared Pearse.

In the crowded barracks that night a prisoner recalled Arthur Griffith's oft-repeated wish, that "England would take her left hand from Ireland's throat and her right hand out of Ireland's pocket," and concluded grimly, "I wish Pearse had told them that."

But another leader on trial that day had chosen rather to quote an Englishman.

" 'Tis sweet and glorious to die for one's country,' sang one of your poets," he reminded his judges. "You would all be proud to die for Britain. I am proud and happy to die for Ireland."

The third man to face that day's rough court-martial had been arrested during a revolt in the 1880s. Fifteen years of the savage nineteenth-century British penal system had failed to break his spirit. But after he received his sentence, he said to his wife, "I'm glad it's death. I've had enough of English jails."

The three were taken that night to grim Kilmainham Prison, whose stones bore the bloodstains of generations of Irish heroes. Next morning, Wednesday, May 3, they were shot.

Before dawn on Thursday, in the bare prison chapel at Kilmainham, another condemned Irish leader was married to his childhood sweetheart. On the morning of Easter Monday he had left a hospital bed to join his comrades. An open wound in his throat was swathed in bandages no whiter than his drawn face. He went to his wedding handcuffed, and a file of British soldiers with drawn bayonets stood all around the chapel walls. An hour later he was executed.

Three more brave Irishmen died with him at Kilmainham. The next day, Friday, there was another victim for the firing squad. No names were published until after the men were shot. None of the dead were released to their families, nor were they allowed Christian burial, but were taken to Arbor Hill Prison and dumped into Maxwell's lime pit. With thousands of Irish patriots still awaiting trial there seemed little hope that Maxwell would stop with a hundred and fifty dead.

But Sinead de Valera would not give up hope. She left her children with a kind Englishwoman who lived next door and hurried into Dublin. She had hidden her husband's American birth certificate from British Intelligence officers who searched her house. At the office of the American consul, she produced it. Whether it would do any good or not she did not know, but when the startled consul had scanned it he said, "Leave this with me. I will see what I can do."

In spite of British censorship, news of the executions was spreading all over the world. Irish in the United States, in the faraway British colonies, even Irish soldiers fighting for

England in the trenches, began recalling all the cruelties and injustices of seven hundred years of British misrule in Ireland.

In England, the Manchester *Guardian* called the executions "atrocities." George Bernard Shaw termed them "slaughter." And when England's Prime Minister was questioned about them in Parliament, an Irish member shouted, "Murder!"

But the courts ground grimly on. Dawn on Monday, May 8, saw four more Irish heroes die at the bullet-scarred Kilmainham wall. That day Eamon de Valera walked to his own court-martial. He had clipped the buttons from his coat and as he walked along he handed them to friends for keepsakes.

The next day, in the United States, members of the Senate requested that President Woodrow Wilson ask clemency for the Irish prisoners from the English Government, but that evening brought news of yet another execution. And the day after that, Wednesday, May 10, Eamon de Valera heard a British officer read his own sentence of death.

He received it calmly. The priest had been allowed to come and hear his confession. He had made his peace with God. There had been one thing on his conscience. The Church forbade membership in secret societies, yet at the urging of a friend, de Valera had joined the secret I.R.B. It had been wrong to do so, he felt now, and he repudiated that membership.

On Thursday morning Eamon de Valera waited to be taken to Kilmainham. No one came for him. There were no executions that day. When his cell door finally opened, it was to admit an official who told him his sentence had been commuted to life imprisonment. This was publicly announced, along with a statement that the trials by court-martial were practically at an end. It took a while for the news to sink in. De Valera had been prepared to die. But now, please God, there would be no more deaths. . . .

He could not bring himself to believe it on the following evening when he heard that two more of his friends were gone. One, a poet, professor, editor of the revolutionary *Irish Freedom,* shot at 3:45 that dreadful Friday morning. The other, James Connolly, the brave leader of Ireland's workingmen, had brought with him to the Rising more than a hundred of Labor's Citizen Army. Severely wounded in the fighting at the Post Office, he had been receiving treatment at the Dublin Castle hospital. He was still too weak and ill to sit up when they carried him that morning to Kilmainham.

A priest walked beside the condemned man. "Will you pray for the men who are about to shoot you?" he asked.

"I will say a prayer for all brave men who do their duty," said James Connolly and, as the rifles were loaded, "Forgive them, for they know not what they do!"

The shots that killed him came in a ragged, sickening volley from the rifles of a completely unnerved firing squad.

This final execution fastened forever on General Maxwell the title by which he would henceforth be known in Ireland: *Bloody Maxwell.*

Lesser officers under his command had done worse. Innocent Irishmen—one of them trying to stop looters—had been murdered by a British captain, their bodies hastily thrown into an unmarked grave. Civilians who had nothing to do with the Rising had been bayoneted to death in front of their families by British soldiers.

The most bitter criticism came from the British themselves. Major Sir Francis Vane denounced the executions, especially that of Connolly, ". . . a badly wounded man taken out, tied to a chair, for he could not stand, and shot like a dog."

It was Major Vane who insisted that the cases of cold-blooded murder by the military be investigated. When he could not persuade his superior officers in the Dublin Command to do anything about them, he went to London and made official protests at the War Office and to the Secretary of War. The latter wired Maxwell, who refused to punish the guilty men. Instead, he dismissed Major Vane from the service. It was not the first time, nor would it be the last, that a conscientious English officer was made to suffer because he demanded justice for the Irish.

One of the British culprits, finally tried, was found criminally insane and sentenced to an institution from which he was quickly, and quietly, released. The English troops who had killed innocent civilians were never identified, much less punished.

Even those Irish who had at first taken the English side began to feel that perhaps the leaders of the Rising had been right. Perhaps complete separation from England was Ireland's only hope for freedom and justice. Soon more of their fellow countrymen began to agree as Maxwell's dragnet brought to the prison cells members of the Irish Volunteers, of Arthur Griffith's independent party, Sinn Fein, and two thousand more men and women, many of whom had resented the Rising as much as the English themselves. Furious at being arrested, sickened by the executions, they listened to rebellious doctrines with open hearts and minds.

They began to ask, "Of what were Pearse and Connolly guilty? Love of country? The desire to see their country free?" World War I was being fought for the right of small countries such as Belgium to defend themselves against an aggressor. Did not Ireland have as much right as Belgium to a government of her own? Similar questions were being asked in the United States, and the English, who had been doing everything in their power to bring America into the war on the side of the Allies, found a disturbing anti-British sentiment building up.

Eamon de Valera might never be sure, but he would always think it was his American birth certificate that had kept him alive. Only one other of the Dublin leaders had escaped death—a beautiful woman, Countess Markievicz, born in Ireland of a wealthy English family, who for a long time had devoted herself to the cause of Irish freedom as leader of the young *Fianna Eireann,* Irish boys under sixteen. During the whole week of the Rising she had fought beside the men in St. Stephen's Green. Perhaps Maxwell flinched at the idea of having a woman shot. Or was public opinion finally bringing so much pressure to bear on the side of the prisoners that he dared not send any more of them to the wall? Whatever the reason, the lovely Irish countess was sent off to a life of hard labor in an English prison.

On the pitching, tossing boat that carried him across the Irish Sea, Eamon de Valera gazed thoughtfully at his manacled hands. He knew how other Irish patriots had been treated in nineteenth-century English prisons. Some of them had died there. Others had gone insane. Had prison conditions improved in the last few years? He doubted it. He and the rest of the Volunteers would simply have to keep their heads, pray for God's help, and hope for release. He did not believe that the English could keep all these Irish prisoners behind bars for the rest of their lives. One day he would go back to his classroom, his mathematics.

In the meantime what would be happening in Ireland? Clearly the Volunteers had asked too much of the Irish people. Or had they simply asked it too soon? In Kingstown, as the handcuffed prisoners were marched to the boat, he had expected more of the catcalls and abuse that had characterized the first days of the Rising. Instead, there had been silence, an occasional muffled cheer, one whispered "God bless you!"

No prisoner was told his destination. Early the next morning de Valera and his companions boarded a train that rocked and jolted behind closely drawn curtains for interminable hours, south to Plymouth. There they were loaded into lorries that climbed along a tree-bordered road to a high, desolate plateau, coming at last to the bleak and forbidding gates of one of England's most notorious prisons: Dartmoor.

" 'Twas in Kilmainham Prison yard our fifteen martyrs died,
  And cold and still in Arbor Hill they are lying side by side.
  But we will yet pay back the debt, for the fire is still alive
  In men who stood through fire and blood with Convict 95!"
      Irish Ballad of 1917

3

OURSELVES
ALONE!

WINDS COLD ENOUGH to chill the heart swept the high Devon plateau. Inside the walls of Dartmoor the cold chilled not only the body but also the spirit. For a month after their arrival the prisoners were closely confined in dank, unheated cells that had not been occupied for years.

German war prisoners were treated better. They were protected by rules of war, their camps inspected by officers of the Red Cross. But the Irish had no one to plead for them. For more than seven hundred years it had been a basic British tenet that Irish rebels who resisted English Government sinned against Divine Law. An Irish political prisoner got the same treatment as a convicted thug or murderer. He was forced to work with convicts, forbidden to talk—as well put an Irishman in a strait jacket as keep him from talking, but so much as a heartening word to a comrade got the speaker three days in solitary, on bread and water.

After a few weeks the Irish looked as villainous as any

felons in Dartmoor. Eamon de Valera fingered his scrubby chin, his hair cropped short by a filthy mechanical clipping machine; he looked at his shoddy, shapeless clothing. Was this part of penal philosophy? If you keep a man looking disreputable, will he lose his self-respect? Will he be easier to handle?

The lack of exercise was even harder to bear. These English jailors did not know the meaning of the word. A man who had been a great runner, whose way of threshing out a problem was on a long, swinging hike to Killiney Bay or across the rounded slopes of Sugar Loaf Mountain, found a slow march around the exercise ring as tiring to his long legs as three paces across his cell, three paces back.

But to de Valera not even the confinement was as bad as the loss of identity. In Dartmoor he was not "Professor" or "Commandant," not Eamon de Valera, but "Convict 95." So long as he remained in prison, he would be not a man but a number.

He refused to accept that. He kept thinking of his family, his pupils, his profession. He spent hours over complicated mathematical problems. He made a special effort to recall in detail everything that led up to the Rising, to analyze the reasons for its failure. A crucial one, no doubt, had been the order against the Sunday maneuvers. But, before Patrick Pearse was shot, he had said, "Do not blame MacNeill. Both he and I did what we thought best for Ireland."

It was ironic that Eoin MacNeill, who had done all he could to stop the Rising, should have been tried and given a sentence as severe as if he had fought alongside the others. He was even sent to Dartmoor. De Valera caught sight of him one evening as he came in with a new bunch of prisoners. How would he be treated here? Prison life was dangerously hard, even for a man who knew himself among friends. Somehow, de Valera felt he must do something that would draw all the Irish prisoners together.

Next morning they lined up for the customary inspection, facing the guards who stood twirling their clubs, alert for the slightest move. De Valera heard steps on the iron stairs, risked a quick glance. It was the new group, with Eoin MacNeill in the lead.

Suddenly the tall de Valera stepped out of the ranks, whirled and faced his friends.

"Irish Volunteers!" he snapped. "Attention! Eyes left!"

It was a salute to MacNeill. Every man obeyed.

"Eyes front!" ordered de Valera and stepped back into the ranks.

It was over before the amazed guards could move. Mutiny such as this called for the lash. They ordered Convict 95 out of line and marched him off to a solitary cell.

Perhaps the incident had been so strange that the chief warden of the prison did not know what to do about it. Nothing happened. Sometime during the afternoon a guard opened the cell door and marched Convict 95 off to join the rest. No one spoke, but the warmth in gray Dartmoor that day had nothing to do with the thermometer.

After that de Valera was generally accepted as leader of the imprisoned Irish. "Dev" they called him affectionately, and although the rule of silence continued to be rigorously enforced, they managed to get his advice on every matter of importance.

Summer brought a wave of oppressive heat. Four hours in the morning, four in the afternoon, the prisoners stitched coarse sandbags, sitting on backless benches in a great bare room with sun pouring down through a ceiling that was mostly glass. After a few hours bending over the bags, de Valera's long back ached like a bad tooth.

As prisoners do, the Irish learned to talk without moving their lips, and their ingenious minds found ways around most of the other regulations. They were not allowed to write letters; in fact, they had no access to pen, ink or paper.

But a team of them managed to steal some ink, fashion a pen and write a long letter that was smuggled out and published by a newspaper in Cork, Ireland. It filled two columns and described in minute detail how Irish prisoners were being treated at Dartmoor.

The chief warden was furious, all the more so because he could not discover how they had accomplished such a feat. No one would talk. Fear of future publicity made him decide on a more lenient policy toward the rebels. A friendly guard subscribed to an Irish newspaper and suddenly they were in contact with home again.

There was news of a fund to help the Volunteers' families, and a scathing letter published in reply to General Maxwell's request that a Catholic bishop discipline priests who had shown sympathy for Irish rebels. Choosing to attack rather than try to defend, the bishop called Maxwell's regime "one of the worst and blackest chapters in the history of the misgovernment of Ireland."

John Redmond and other Irish members of Parliament were demanding Maxwell's recall and lifting of the martial law he had imposed on Ireland. Redmond was also insisting that the hundreds of Irish who had been deported without trial be immediately released from British detention camps. And those such as de Valera who had taken an active part in the Rising should, Redmond thought, be treated as political prisoners rather than as criminals.

No one seemed to pay any attention to him. The long, hot days of June and July stretched uneventfully into August days that might not be quite so long but were even hotter in the blistering workroom at Dartmoor. And Eamon de Valera's unhappiness was compounded by the trial in London of his comrade Sir Roger Casement.

The charge against Casement was, of course, treason. The English tried him, convicted him, sentenced him to be hanged. Not content with his death, they blackened his memory by unsavory accusations against his character. De Valera, who knew Casement to be the most idealistic of men, burned with an anger all the more bitter because he was helpless to defend his friend. But Casement's true character showed in the speech he made to the court.

When he was captured, Casement had been on his way to Dublin to try to stop the Rising. He refused to plead thus, choosing rather to speak of his love for Ireland, to identify himself with other patriots who had laid down their lives for her.

"If this be the cause I stand here today indicted for, and convicted for sustaining," he concluded, "then I stand in a goodly company and a right noble succession!"

The last of sixteen leaders of the Rising executed, he was hanged in Pentonville Prison; his body, like those of the others, was thrown into an unmarked, unconsecrated grave within the prison walls.

The British could scarcely be blamed for wishing that the whole Irish nation could be disposed of in like fashion. When a renegade Englishman was condemned to life imprisonment at hard labor, he usually went to prison, did the labor and obeyed the rules. Not so the Irish. They refused to recognize British authority, inside or outside prison. To the last man, they stuck to that principle. They not only fought their captors, they laughed at them. They succeeded in organizing themselves, in choosing a leader—as the men of Dartmoor chose de Valera—whose orders they carried out. The frustrated wardens could not even discover how such orders were transmitted.

After a time de Valera and some of the other Dartmoor prisoners who had been losing weight were given an extra six ounces of bread a day. Dev felt others needed the nourishment more than he did, so one afternoon he tossed his small loaf across a dim hall into another cell.

A guard spied him, yelled, "Hey you—none of that!" and

both Dev and the man he had tried to befriend went to the solitary cells. Dev preferred to go on a hunger strike rather than submit to bread-and-water punishment. That was too much for the chief warden. He threw up his hands and ordered the transfer of his stubborn prisoner.

Dev's example continued to inspire the men left behind. They gloried in his defiance, liking especially to recall the day he had refused to salute when the chief warden came into the workroom. Several guards started to converge on him, but suddenly he rose, brushed by them and in his most dignified manner said to the astounded warden, "Please understand that I have as much contempt for a bully when I am standing up as when I am seated."

Some of the English leaders in government began to admit that they did not understand the Irish. The Prime Minister said that his government had made some stupid blunders in its dealings with them. Lloyd George chimed in with a pious wish that something be done to improve the political situation in Ireland. Something *must* be done. If the great war were ever to be won, England must have the help of the United States. Yet in November 1916, Woodrow Wilson was re-elected President with the slogan HE KEPT US OUT OF WAR!

Soon General Maxwell was called home from Ireland. A month later, Lloyd George became Prime Minister of England. It did not bode well for Ireland that Sir Edward Carson, bane of the southern Irish, stayed on in the British Cabinet; that Bonar Law, another supporter of the rebels in Belfast and leader of the House of Commons, also became a Cabinet member. But at the moment public opinion seemed to be tipping the balance in Ireland's favor.

"It may be dangerous to let the Irish internees go home," said the Chief Secretary for Ireland, "but it is even more so to detain them longer."

Six hundred untried prisoners were released in time to get home for Christmas. The rest were held only a few days longer. But Convict 95 and his companions seemed as far as ever from freedom. Dev had been shifted once again and, with 120 Irish prisoners, was now at Lewes in Sussex, south of London.

The rules here were far less strict than at Dartmoor, but the puzzled English found that if they gave Irish prisoners permission to talk, they were apt to sing at the top of their lungs. And their fiendish ingenuity could drive any English jailor out of his mind. He never knew what was going to happen next.

There was nothing for it but to crack down on them. No more talking except during exercise periods. And from now on, they were to obey all orders without question. Without question, mind you!

The prisoners were lined up to hear the ultimatum. The officer had no sooner stopped reading than Eamon de Valera stepped forward. He was not allowed to speak. The prisoners were marched back to their cells and the order passed along: If anyone has anything to say, he must ask for an audience with the chief warden himself.

Unbeknownst to the prison authorities, the Irish prisoners had established a chain of communication with their compatriots at home. Policies agreed on in Dublin were made known to de Valera and now he proceeded to put an important one into practice. It was time, he told his companions, to make a formal demand that they be treated either as political prisoners or as prisoners of war. They must refuse to work as convicts, to associate with convicts. "Tomorrow we begin," said Dev. "No one marches until I give the word."

Next morning the chief warden appeared as they lined up on the exercise field.

"March," came the order.

No one moved.

The warden's face went white. De Valera stepped forward and handed him a paper.

"I am demanding that we Irish Volunteers be treated as prisoners of war," said Dev formally. "We refuse any longer to accept convict status."

He stepped back. The warden stared. Two officials whispered for a moment, then said to the guards, "Take them back to their cells."

They stayed in their cells until Saturday. Then they were asked, "If you are allowed to go to Mass tomorrow, will you promise not to make any demonstrations or try to escape?"

Most of them were devout Catholics who received communion every Sunday. But even though it meant being deprived of the Sacraments, they would make no promises.

On Monday Dev told the Volunteers that he had given the authorities three days to meet Irish demands. If they were still locked in at the end of that period, each man was to start breaking up his cell. The first night, the windows. Next night, the spy holes in the doors. The third night, the lamp screens. . . .

At the end of the third day Dev gave the signal. Then came the crash of breaking glass and wave after wave of cheers. The noise could be heard for blocks, and from all over Lewes people came running.

The night after, the Irish demolished the spy holes; the next saw the last of the lamp screens. Then it was every man for himself. One prisoner chipped and pried at a brick in his cell wall until he worked it loose and, of course, found those next to it even easier to dislodge. Before he stopped, he had made three small cells into one big one.

That was when Lewes' chief warden got rid of Convict 95. And he shipped off the rest of the Irish as fast as he could, until they were scattered among a half-dozen English prisons.

One of the last Volunteers to go was the dignified Eoin

MacNeill. The day the Irish writer Bob Brennan left he reported seeing the professor sitting on his window sill with legs dangling outside. He had taken off his shoes, thrust his bare feet between the bars, then replaced the shoes, so he could not be dragged from his cell. A professor behaving like a schoolboy! Small wonder that prison guards resigned and chief wardens found their hair turning white overnight.

Through an incredibly bitter winter the Irish prisoners fought their grim battle. And at home, the released internees, headed by Sinn Fein's Arthur Griffith and the burly young ex-bank teller Michael Collins, started the political fight against John Redmond, leader of the Irish delegates to the British Parliament.

The British had blamed the 1916 Rising on Arthur Griffith's Sinn Fein party. That was doing Griffith an injustice, because he had never believed in violence. But by the time the internees came home they were accustomed to hearing themselves called "Shinners," or "Sinn Feiners." Gradually the name began to be applied to men who cherished widely varying ideas about Ireland's connection with, or independence from, England.

When a by-election was called that snowy February of 1917 to fill a vacancy in the Irish delegation to the British Parliament, this Sinn Fein coalition nominated the father of a young man who had been executed after the Rising. To the consternation of Redmond and the British, the Sinn Fein candidate won by more than thirteen hundred votes.

At once Dublin Castle ordered the arrest of twenty-six internees, charging them with such desperate crimes as "flying the flag of Irish rebellion" (Pearse's tricolor), "using words and phrases that might incite others to rebellion," and even "singing disloyal songs."

And Ireland was threatened with a military draft.

The war in Europe had not been going well for England and her allies. The battle for Verdun had raged from February 1916 to December, taking such a toll of lives that re-inforcements for the armies were needed desperately. The flow of enlistments in Ireland had choked to a trickle after the Rising in late April. The Belfast leader Sir Edward Carson had long been urging that Irishmen be drafted into the British Army.

Until now, Lloyd George had refused. America, he said, was hanging in the balance. Although President Wilson had broken off diplomatic relations with Germany, England was still unable to persuade the United States to enter the war. A military draft in Ireland would infuriate Irish-Americans, might weigh the scale of American sentiment even more heavily against a decision to fight for England.

And an Irish draft could cause serious trouble in Canada, Australia, and South Africa, all of whom had many citizens of Irish descent.

"They would say," cried Lloyd George dramatically, " 'You are fighting for the freedom of nationalities. What right have you to take this nation by the ear and drag it into war against its will?' "

But Lloyd George was trying to do something far worse to Ireland than drag her into England's war. He was trying to divide the country. To placate Irish-Americans he was pretending the deepest sympathy for Ireland, saying that his government was prepared to grant her Home Rule at once. But he was offering self-government only to "that part of Ireland which clearly demanded it." He had no intention of "forcing the leaders of the British Ascendancy in Ulster to accept Home Rule." He had made that clear when he took Carson and Bonar Law into his Cabinet.

Lloyd George knew very well that the Irish would never consent to partition of their country, that an overwhelming majority even of those living in Ulster would vote against it. He had made his proposal to impress the people of the United

States, and his ruse was successful. In April 1917, that country declared war on Germany.

Even after this, the British Ambassador in Washington kept urging his government to settle the entire Irish question. Otherwise, he said, it would be continually cited as proof that England was not, as she claimed, fighting this war for the independence of small nations. But Lloyd George was satisfied with matters as they stood—until another vacancy in the Irish delegation to Parliament required the calling of another by-election to fill it.

This time Sinn Fein proposed the name of John McGuinness, an Irish prisoner still in Lewes.

PUT HIM IN TO GET HIM OUT! said big black posters on every wall.

The campaign was fought, not against the Parliamentary candidate, but against the threat of Partition. In spite of the fact that Redmond and the other Irish members had walked out of the House of Commons at the very mention of the word, the Irish people felt their representatives in the British Parliament had almost been tricked into agreeing to the division of Ireland.

Again the Sinn Fein candidate won—only by virtue of three recounts and thirty-seven votes, to be sure, but the English recognized it as a serious defeat and the Irish set bonfires blazing on every hilltop in Ireland.

PARTITION IS AS DEAD AS A DOOR-NAIL, said a banner headline in the pro-British *Irish Times*.

Some said that Lloyd George was conniving even when he slept. Now he produced a new plan. He would call an Irish Convention, he said, to discuss settlement of all problems and submit to the English Cabinet proposals for the future government of Ireland *within the Empire*.

Arthur Griffith recognized that the Convention was just another of Lloyd George's tricks. Sinn Fein refused to have

any part in it. To make their stand perfectly clear, they said:
Only IF the Convention would discuss Irish independence and

IF England would solemnly promise Ireland, the United States, and the European Powers to ratify any decision of the Convention, and

IF the Convention were made up of men chosen by the Irish people in a free election, and

IF the Irish in English jails were given the treatment due them as prisoners of war

would Sinn Fein come into said Convention!

All Ireland and some of the English saw how wise the Sinn Fein leaders had been when Lloyd George announced how Convention delegates were to be chosen. Even the London *Times* cried "Hand-picked!" Fifteen were to be named by the English Crown; forty-seven more were to be mayors and chairmen of public bodies in Ireland (all, of course, elected long before the Rising); and the remaining thirty-nine were divided among Chambers of Commerce, organized labor, political parties and the Catholic Church. Sinn Fein, the strongest political party in Ireland, was offered five seats.

Eamon de Valera was being kept informed of all these developments. And the Sinn Fein leaders were watching him, marking his influence among the Irish prisoners.

On June 10, 1917, a tremendous crowd gathered in Dublin to demand better treatment for those prisoners. Two speakers who addressed the meeting were promptly arrested. That set off a riot. The police used clubs on the crowd and were attacked in return by blows from hurley sticks. One of those blows killed a police inspector. A few months earlier, everyone there would have been hauled off to jail. But the English remembered the two elections already won by Sinn Fein. A third would soon be held in County Clare. Should Sinn Fein run a candidate, any further arrests by the British might win him the election.

Five days later the British announced: "In order to secure a favorable atmosphere for the Irish Convention, the government has decided to release all Irish prisoners."

De Valera was gathered with the rest at London's Pentonville Prison. It was the dirtiest jail they had seen, its cells crawling with hungry lice. On the exercise ground, the Irish were fitted out with civilian clothes. Before they left the prison, some of them managed to make their way to the spot where Roger Casement was buried, to kneel there and say a prayer, to promise that one day they would bring his body home to Ireland.

Convict 95—no—Eamon de Valera—found that his shoddy new suit fitted his long, rangy body not much better than the prison clothing had, but what did that matter—he was free.

Yet, as the prison gates closed behind him, did another kind of bondage lie ahead? Someone thrust a telegram into his hands.

"We have chosen you," he read, "to represent Sinn Fein in a by-election in East Clare."

"Up de Valera! he's the champion of the right,
  We'll follow him to battle 'neath the Orange, Green
      and White,
  And when next we challenge England we'll beat her
      in the fight,
  And we'll crown de Valera king of Ireland!"
    Irish Ballad of 1917

4

PLEDGED TO
IRELAND

IN THE LAST SCENE of a play by the Irish poet William Butler
Yeats, Ireland—portrayed as the "Poor Old Woman" of Penal
Days—speaks to a young man about to be married, calling
him to come with her. And although she promises nothing
but sorrow and defeat, when she leaves he is drawn irre-
sistibly to follow. As his abandoned bride sits beside the
hearth weeping, the groom's young brother comes in and his
distressed mother asks, "Did you see a Poor Old Woman just
now, going down the path?"

"No," says the boy, "but I saw a beautiful young woman,
and she had the walk of a queen!"

Through the short play the strange woman sings the praise
of Irish heroes who through the centuries had turned their
backs on loving brides and warm firesides to go out for Ireland into the gray rain, plodding lonely through the dark
nights—most of those heroes still young and strong when

their necks were stretched on a gibbet or when they faced the rifles of a firing squad.

> *They shall be remembered forever;*
> *They shall be living forever;*
> *They shall be speaking forever;*
> *The people shall hear them forever. . . .*

When those words were spoken from a Dublin stage, cheers rocked the theater even in the apathetic days before the 1916 Rising. And after the execution of its heroes a spate of poems honored their dream of Irish freedom and their readiness to die for it. The Volunteers returning after more than a year in English prisons were to find the ashes of apathy blown away, the red coals of patriotism burning as hot as they had ever burned in the days of Sarsfield or the 1798 rebellion.

On the morning of June 18, 1917, standing at the rail of the cross-Channel mail boat, Eamon de Valera had no idea what awaited him in this Ireland whose shores rose green and beautiful out of the sea. The hundred or more of his companions were singing their homesick hearts out in the "Soldier's Song":

> *Sons of the Gael,*
> *Men of the Pale,*
> *The long-watched day is breaking. . . .*

They fell silent as the boat came alongside the Kingstown pier. Other passengers filed ashore. The men with pale faces and closely cropped heads waited for de Valera to give the order before they marched double file down the gangway.

Along the Dublin quays a singing, cheering crowd had waited through the night, expecting a boat from Liverpool to dock there with their heroes. At daybreak, when the news was passed that the prisoners were instead landing at Kingstown, the waiting throng surged toward Westland Row Station. When the train pulled in, a cordon of Irish Volunteers was needed to hold the crowd in check.

The tall, dark figure of Eamon de Valera loomed above his companions, brown eyes searching the crowd for someone he knew. His friends saw a sober stranger with new lines in his thin, clean-shaven face, a firmer set to his full lips than they had remembered. But his smile was warm, his handclasp firm. It was difficult for Dev to conceal his emotion. Remembering the sullen crowds of last year's Rising, he was stunned by this amazing, tumultuous welcome. He found it hard to believe when someone directed him toward a group of city officials who had come to greet the prisoners.

The ceremonies made him uneasy. He wished he could get through the crowd and go home, but there was a further delay. He had to join the group of Volunteer officers, meeting at that moment to draft a letter to President Wilson and the Congress of the United States.

Although they had been able to maintain contact with Volunteers in Ireland, little news had filtered into their prison cells.

"We, the undersigned," they wrote now, "who have been held in English prisons and have been dragged from dungeon to dungeon, in heavy chains, cut off since Easter Week, 1916, from all intercourse with the outside world, have just had an opportunity of seeing the printed text of President Wilson's [recent] statement. . . ."

They quoted from it: "No people must be forced under a sovereignty under which it does not wish to live."

In their message the Volunteer officers claimed for the Irish people the right to defend themselves against external aggression, external interference, external control. And they declared flatly, "We are engaged and mean to engage ourselves in practical means for establishing this right!"

Then they identified themselves, these men just released from English prisons, as officers of a military force whose aim was to secure the complete liberation of the Irish nation. First to sign, in his clear, firm hand, was Eamon de Valera.

Not until then could he go home to his family, to welcome the baby son he had never seen, born the previous November and named, as had been his wish, for Roger Casement.

The older boys were stanch little fellows. How they had grown—and Maureen, too. She was a bit shy, standing off for a long look at him. It would take a few days for the children to grow accustomed to having a father again. And would he have even a few days before going off to Clare? The election was only three weeks away. What was Sinead to think of this new separation? She and the children had already suffered greatly. Any woman might feel that he should stay at home now and take care of his family.

Sinead de Valera was a little woman, the top of her hair not quite reaching as high as her husband's shoulder. But she had a great heart and, as some British Intelligence officers had discovered, she could be as fearless and loyal as any soldier, without losing one bit of her femininity. She loved her husband. She yearned to keep him at home. But her Dev was head of his house. He must do as he thought best.

Women the world over, however, are often more practical than men, and to any practical mind the by-elections of 1917 made little sense. Both Sinn Fein candidates already elected this year vowed they would not sit in the British Parliament, although it was vacancies in that Parliament that the by-elections were supposed to fill. For what, then, were Sinn Feiners being elected? To sit in an Irish Parliament here in Dublin! Such a Parliament did not exist? Well, what's the matter with you, have you no faith . . . ?

Sinead de Valera had no faith whatever in politicians, but she had a world of it in her husband. If anyone could make such a visionary scheme work, he could. It must have been a powerful force indeed that made Dev, who had always disliked politics, consent to run for office.

On the day he left for Clare, Sinead, who knew her poetry and her theater, may well have been reminded of Yeats' poetic notion. Ireland a Poor Old Woman? To Irish sons and husbands she would forever be a beautiful young woman with the walk of a queen!

It was to no romantic high adventure that Eamon de Valera traveled, but to three weeks of sober, hard campaigning. But the journey southwestward from Dublin is one to stir the heart of any man. The sun- and cloud-dappled Wicklow Mountains were at his back; a vast, rolling central plain stretched before him. In the warm June sun, the green of trees and fields and hedges was almost too brilliant to look upon. It must have been a dazzling brilliance for eyes whose horizons for more than a year had been bounded by the drab gray walls of prison.

Not far outside Dublin is The Curragh, five thousand acres of emerald turf. Home of a British military garrison, it is more famed for its centuries of Irish horse racing. Once past its wide expanse of open grassland, the roads are bordered by scenery-hiding hedges and walls, but through gaps in them the country-bred eye may catch glimpses of yellowing hayfields or the pink blossoming froth of apple trees, a church spire reaching toward heaven, perhaps a black cloud of rooks diving and swooping above the ruins of a castle.

Every town and village along the way is a monument to Irish courage, a miracle of Irish survival. Plundered and burned in the fourteenth century, many of them were sacked again in the seventeenth, and later in that century captured by Cromwell. Yet within another hundred years Irishmen had not hesitated to come out and fight here in the ill-starred insurrection of 1798. In one village square, a fine Celtic cross marks the spot where a Catholic priest was hanged for his part in that rebellion. And south of it is the town whose name was made infamous in 1366 by the Statutes of Kilken which set the death penalty for many offenses, among th daring to marry an Irishwoman.

Long before the tragic years of conquest, this ancient land was visited by St. Patrick. In A.D. 470 the great St. Brigid founded a monastery at Kildare. And the High Kings of Ireland reigned there in the days about which the old storyteller of Bruree used to sing. Beautiful country, fertile country—why should not the British have coveted it, wanted to keep it?

At the end of the 140-mile ride from Dublin is Ennis, county seat for Clare. Eamon de Valera felt quite at home in Ennis. His Uncle Patrick's farm was not far south, across the Shannon. The countrymen who came in from their small rocky fields to hear Dev speak were like his Uncle Patrick's neighbors. Life was not easy in Limerick or Clare, but these were a self-reliant folk who thought for themselves.

If it made little sense to campaign for a seat in the British Parliament he promised not to fill, Clare was an ideal place to do it. Here the Catholic Daniel O'Connell (for whom the wide Dublin bridge across the Liffey was named) campaigned for a seat in that same Parliament at a time no Catholic was allowed to sit in it.

"I will never give up my religion," vowed O'Connell.

Clare elected him. He refused the test oath which would have meant repudiating his faith. He was seated anyway, and so was broken the ban against Catholic members of Parliament.

Unlike O'Connell, de Valera was no orator. The first crowds who gathered to hear the tall, thin man in the gray-green uniform of the Rising cheered the uniform more than the man or what he said. But the Irish farmers and small shopkeepers liked Dev's straightforward, honest way of speaking. With regard to the differences of opinion within his party he said earnestly, "We want an Irish Republic. If Ireland has her freedom, a Republic is, I believe, the most likely form of government. But if the people want some other form of government, as long as it is an Irish government, I would not put in a word against it."

And County Clare liked it when Dev introduced Professor Eoin MacNeill from the platform.

"MacNeill—he would be the man who tried to stop the Rising, wouldn't he?" said one.

"He would," said another, "but de Valera vowed he wouldn't come at all unless MacNeill were allowed to come too. De Valera says we Irish have to stick together."

His fair-minded listeners were further impressed when de Valera had a Sinn Fein election poster torn from the walls of Ennis. It was not right, he protested, to picture a member of the opposition party as a hangman.

Dev could not hope to cover the district by himself in such a short period, but presently he had plenty of assistance. Young Volunteers in Dublin got out their bicycles for the long trek to Ennis, and sang as they rode, "Soldiers are we, whose lives are pledged to Ireland . . ." On arrival, they fanned out over the countryside to tell their enthusiastic story of de Valera. They met plenty of arguments. The opposition candidate was pounding away, trying to frighten people by the threat of English guns.

"Clare voters do not want to see their sons shot down in a futile and insane attempt to establish an Irish Republic!" he cried.

Many thought him right. Ireland's best friend in the world, the United States, was fighting alongside the English in the great European war. So were hundreds of young men from Clare. The British were in firm control here, with posts of the Royal Irish Constabulary in every village. Cobwebs and moonbeams were more substantial than this dream of an independent Irish Republic!

But the people of County Clare cherished a centuries-long

tradition of freedom. They were proud of another tradition, being the straw in the wind of change. Just as in the United States people say, "As Maine goes, so goes the nation," so it was boasted here, "What happens today in Clare will be all over Ireland tomorrow."

On July 10, Eamon de Valera got more than twice the number of votes given his Parliamentary opponent.

It had been more of a crusade than a political campaign. On election night Dev ordered the bar closed in the hotel where he had his headquarters. And when he thanked the crowd that had voted for him, he called the election a monument to the glorious men of Easter Week, who had died for Ireland.

Fires flared from every hilltop in Clare that night and all over Ireland people rejoiced. The shocked and disbelieving English felt something must be done; their idea of something was, as usual, a show of force. Police fired into one cheering crowd and killed a man. Anyone who dared fly the tricolor was arrested; many were fined and imprisoned. But the Irish people continued to fly the flag and they did not seem at all afraid to show their sympathy for those who had been arrested.

The prisoners needed sympathy. That late summer of 1917 saw them fighting the same bitter battle in Irish jails the Volunteers had fought in English ones, demanding to be recognized as political prisoners, not convicts. When this demand was refused, they went on hunger strike.

Thomas Ashe, one of their outstanding leaders, died as a result of being forcibly fed. There was such an uproar in Dublin that authorities did not dare interfere when Volunteers dressed Thomas Ashe's body in his officer's uniform and took him to lie in state at the City Hall with a Volunteer guard of honor. Thousands filed past to pay their respects. Thousands more followed him to his grave, every last one of them wearing the banned tricolor badge of orange, white, and green. He was given a full-dress military funeral that ended with the sounding of "The Last Post" and a salute of three rifle volleys over his grave.

This demonstration brought better treatment, temporarily, for the remaining prisoners, but the British seemed to have short memories. Soon they were again rating all the Irish as criminals, and once again a hunger strike was called.

Eamon de Valera had returned from Clare to plunge into political affairs with the same single-minded concentration he had once devoted to mathematics. At his suggestion William Cosgrave was named to contest yet another by-election. Cosgrave had fought in the Rising, had been condemned to death; his sentence, like Dev's had been commuted to life imprisonment. It was an unbeatable combination that summer of 1917. But when Cosgrave won, the infuriated British sent police and soldiers into houses, parish halls, even the homes of priests to search for hidden arms. And once again, British law was different for Northeast Ulster and the rest of Ireland. Only Sinn Fein guns were confiscated. Arms and ammunition belonging to the pro-British "Ulster Specials" were untouched.

But there were even more serious matters to concern Dev than election campaigns and British oppression. The divisions in the ranks of those the British called Sinn Fein were threatening to widen into chasms. Under the Sinn Fein umbrella were two major factions—a moderate wing headed by Arthur Griffith, and an all-or-nothing Irish Republic group whose outspoken leader was Cathal Brugha. Each group was infiltrated by the secret Irish Republican Brotherhood, whose most influential members at this point were Michael Collins, Harry Boland and Austin Stack. Both Dev and Brugha would have been happy to see the I.R.B. abolished, but its members continued to work behind the scenes.

Since the 1890s Arthur Griffith had been preaching the doctrine of Sinn Fein: separation from England, an Irish

Parliament. More than any other writer's, his fiery phrases had stirred the Irish people to rebellion. In spite of his disapproval of armed resistance, during the Rising he had made his way to the beleaguered Post Office and reported for duty. Pearse sent him home again, saying he could do more for Ireland with his pen than with any gun. Griffith had spent a year in an English internment camp. Now he looked skeptically at the idea of an Irish Republic, feeling that Ireland's best hope was some sort of Home Rule arrangement.

Cathal Brugha preferred action to words. During the Rising he had defended a vitally important position single-handed and was so riddled with bullets they said of him forever after that he jingled when he walked. Sure he was dying, the British had not even brought him up for trial. A man of stern and uncompromising ideals, he had a ferocious temper and said once of himself, "When roused, I'm no angel!"

Michael Collins, younger than Brugha or Griffith, came from a West Cork family with a long tradition of Irish patriotism. He had worked in London as a postal clerk, then in a banking firm, had come home to join the Rising, and fought in the Post Office with the main body of Pearse's command. Harry Boland, a brilliant young man with the most infectious laugh in Dublin and a personality to match, was to a great extent under Collins' influence at this time. So probably was Austin Stack.

These, then, were the men Eamon de Valera strove to draw together—each with widely differing ideas not only about how to achieve Irish independence, but also about what kind of government would be best for Ireland.

It took a true diplomat to reconcile them. Dev thought he had a formula that might do it.

"We aim," he said at a meeting with these men, "to secure international recognition of Ireland as an independent Irish Republic."

A rare smile appeared on Cathal Brugha's face.

"Having achieved that status," Dev went on, "the Irish people may by referendum choose their own form of government."

That made Arthur Griffith's eyes gleam behind his steel-rimmed spectacles and suddenly, where there had been bitter disagreement, there was harmony.

They called a Sinn Fein Convention and drew up a Constitution for Ireland that made the British goggle when they read it. How dared these Irish set up their own National Assembly, plan protective tariffs for Irish industries, a consular service, their own courts, even a well-worked-out system of social reform!

The Constitution was approved unanimously by the Convention. The next order of business was to choose a president. Because of Arthur Griffith's long record of devotion to the cause of Irish freedom, many felt that he should have the honor. Count Plunkett, who had won that first by-election in 1917 under the Sinn Fein banner, also had strong support for the position. But he and Arthur Griffith shared a desire for Irish unity which transcended self-interest. They withdrew in favor of Eamon de Valera, and he was made president by acclamation.

A few weeks later, he was also elected president of the Irish Volunteers, so the military and political forces of the country were now united under the same head.

In London, Prime Minister Lloyd George had taken notice of de Valera's rise to power. Referring to his election to Parliament the preceding July, Lloyd George commented: "I have read the speeches of the honorable member from East Clare. They are not excited, and so far as language is concerned, they are not violent. They are plain, deliberate, and I might also say *cold-blooded* incitements to rebellion. . . . This is not a case of violent, abusive, and excitable language. It is the case of a man of great ability, of considerable influence, deliberately going down to the district to stir people up to rebellion against the authorities."

He would have loved to throw de Valera into jail again, but it would be a most embarrassing thing to do. All Dev's speeches supported the principle of self-determination for nations. That was President Wilson's principle, and Lloyd George had himself endorsed it.

Then, too, de Valera had the backing of hundreds of thousands of people throughout Ireland. During every weekend he held parades and addressed meetings of the Volunteers. And in every speech he hammered away at the same theme:

"If England is out for the cause of small nations, she should prove it by giving Ireland her freedom!"

Lloyd George's Irish Convention, in which Sinn Fein took no part, had been dragging along for three months in Dublin. Now Lloyd George accused de Valera of trying to smash it.

"I am not trying to smash anything but the British connection," said Dev. He had warned the Irish people long ago that the Convention was nothing but a trap, that they should refuse "to walk into the spider's parlor." England needed no Convention. She could set up Home Rule in Ireland at any moment, if she were really in earnest.

The Convention had accomplished exactly what Lloyd George intended it should, quieting those who criticized England for her Irish policy. As a member of Parliament graphically put it, the Convention was "a bone thrown to a snarling dog. The longer there was anything to gnaw, the longer would the dog keep quiet."

But now John Redmond warned the Prime Minister: "If the Convention fails, you will have to govern Ireland by the naked sword."

No one could say that it failed. Its deliberations and conclusions were simply ignored. To Lloyd George's consternation, his hand-picked Irish Convention showed an amazing unity. Its report showed a vote of 73 per cent against the partition of Ireland. Hastily Lloyd George thrust the report in his pocket and said he hadn't time to read it. He was busy with another plan. And this one was to bring countless thousands to the standard of Sinn Fein and the leadership of Eamon de Valera.

"We'll set Ireland free from the sod to the sky on you,
   There's a surprise for you, David Lloyd George!"
      Irish Song of 1918

5

CONSCRIPTION

As THE WET green winter of 1917–1918 wore into a wetter spring, the great European war was going badly for England and her allies. A sweeping attack by the Germans cut the British Fifth Army to pieces and put France in the gravest peril she had experienced since the Battle of the Marne. The Germans bombarded Paris, aimed another great offensive at the British lines in Flanders, and threatened Ypres. There was a dire need for reinforcements in the ranks of the Allies.

Lloyd George's plan was to take care of this shortage of fighting men. If the Irish would not volunteer for the Army, they must be drafted. He sent an Irish conscription bill to the House of Commons.

Every Irish member of Parliament voted against it.

"You may as well declare war on Ireland and be done with it," said one of them. "And it will be a futile war. It will take three English Army Corps to get one Irish Corps out of the country. And in the process, you will destroy the Irish Parliamentary party. You are driving millions of the best men of our race to turn away their eyes from this Parliament forever!"

When the bill passed in mid-April, the Irish members packed up and went home. Two days later the Lord Mayor of Dublin called a meeting that brought together at the Mansion House men who had been fighting one another politically, but were now joining forces against the British.

Again it was de Valera who managed to unite those of widely differing backgrounds and personalities. The simplicity of his pledge against the military draft appealed to all. After some discussion they agreed that it should be solemnly taken in every parish in the country. The pledge read:

Denying the right of the British Government to enforce compulsory service in this country, we pledge ourselves solemnly to one another to resist Conscription by the most effective means at our disposal.

Out of the meeting also came a unanimous declaration that the conscription bill was in direct violation of the rights of small nations to rule themselves—rights Prime Minister Lloyd George himself had declared an essential condition for world peace.

It was not enough, thought de Valera, for political leaders alone to advocate so defiant a move. If the deeply religious people of Ireland were to put their whole hearts into their resistance they must have the sanction of their spiritual leaders as well. The Lord Mayor with de Valera and three Irish members of Parliament appeared at a conference of the Catholic bishops, begging them to issue a public statement against conscription. The bishops responded with a rousing "The Irish people have a right to resist by every means that are consonant with the laws of God!"

On Sunday, April 21, de Valera's pledge was signed everywhere in Ireland except in pro-British strongholds. On Tuesday, labor called a one-day strike that, except in Belfast, closed every shop and factory in Ireland. Trains and streetcars came to a halt. In the south and west no newspapers appeared. Bars were closed. Hotel guests had to serve themselves. Even the taxis refused to take passengers.

The Irish had thrown down the gauntlet. Either England must set Ireland free or govern her by force.

It must be force, decided Lloyd George and his government. They called home from Ireland Lord Wimbourne and every other English official who might have any sympathy whatsoever for the Irish, and appointed Field Marshal Lord French "His Majesty's Lord Lieutenant General, and Governor-General of Ireland." Thus, as in the period after the Rising, a military man was placed in complete charge of the country.

"If they will leave me alone," he said, referring no doubt to the politicians, "I can do what is necessary. I shall notify a date before which recruits must offer themselves in the various districts. If they do not come, we will fetch them."

"There will be shooting," warned Lloyd George. "Be sure that it is the rebels who shoot first, so we can lay the blame on them."

Lord French would be assisted by regular British Army divisions and by the efficient Royal Irish Constabulary, the police. Practically all the latter were native Irish, but through the years they had been so completely indoctrinated by the British that almost to a man they were loyal to England. Michael Collins, however, had begun to build up in their ranks a highly efficient system of espionage.

Not long after the arrival of Lord French, a detective in the "G" (political intelligence) division, came to Collins with a list of Irishmen slated for immediate arrest. Eamon de Valera was one of them.

What should they do—hide? Dev did not think that a good idea. Why not let themselves be taken? Irish resentment at seeing their leaders arrested would give Sinn Fein an advantage in the by-election coming up in Cavan. And there were plenty of men who could carry on in their place.

Dev had reason for his faith in his countrymen. Competent Irishmen seemed to appear wherever they were needed in these troubled times. At the beginning of the year, the shadow of hunger was beginning to fall across the country. British officials scoffed at the notion, but the famine years of the 1840s were still as grisly fresh in Irish memories as if they had happened yesterday. Although the English Food Controller had been overruling every effort to conserve supplies in Ireland, the Sinn Fein leaders calculated that there was only enough food to last six months.

Eamon de Valera and Arthur Griffith had agreed that more wheat should be raised, that it was foolish to import grain which they could just as well grow themselves. Some of the great tracts of Irish land used only for grazing could be put to better use, they thought, if it were planted to wheat.

As soon as the ground could be worked, Sinn Fein had come up with a plan that would not only produce wheat for bread, but would also satisfy the people of the western counties who wanted to farm. And it certainly would demonstrate the power and efficiency of Sinn Fein.

Young men belonging to local Sinn Fein clubs cleared the cattle from certain grazing lands, divided the land into small plots, leased them to farmers, collected the rents and paid them to the owner of the land. To dramatize the movement, on their way to plow the fields men marched in parade, escorted by crowds bright with tricolor flags, noisy with fife and drum. There were some arrests, but many crowds were so large the police thought it better not to interfere.

Even after County Clare was proclaimed a military area, the Sinn Fein clubs continued to function. British troops came in. Letters and telegrams were censored, as were local newspapers. One of the latter was forced to stop publication.

In Dublin the Sinn Fein Food Controller ordered his men

to seize a drove of pigs being driven to the docks for export, to take them to a nearby slaughterhouse, process them there, and sell the meat to local butchers. What made Dev so proud of his men was the orderly manner in which they carried out these extraordinary maneuvers.

Ireland had never been more free of serious crime. The jails, of course, were full, but that was because the British went about arresting people who were only "suspected *to be about to commit an act* that would breach the peace." Two hundred thirteen such arrests were made in one month.

For some time all Sinn Fein leaders had been living under the constant threat of arrest, but Eamon de Valera had told the British, "We will not be frightened. If we do not succeed we will pass on the fight as a sacred duty to those who will come after us." The steady gaze of his brown eyes, his erect soldier's stance, and the earnestness with which he spoke convinced them that he meant exactly what he said.

Until now top men of Sinn Fein had gone unhindered about their business, but Michael Collins was sure that his informant had the correct information, that now every Sinn Feiner boasting any authority at all was to be taken into custody. Most of the men whose names were on the list agreed with Dev—let the British arrest them. Michael Collins and Cathal Brugha strongly disagreed.

De Valera did not even get a chance to go home and say goodbye to Sinead and his children. He was taken as he got off the train at Greystones. He had been a free man for less than a year, but he showed neither fear nor uneasiness as he walked between his armed captors to the boat at Kingstown. Someone in the watching crowd recognized him and shouted, "Give us a message!"

Dev turned and called back, "Be calm and confident."

Before the boat pulled away for England seventy-three more of Ireland's leaders were brought aboard. Somewhere out in the darkness a voice was singing, "When next we challenge England, we'll beat her in the fight, and we'll crown de Valera king of Ireland!" It was a ballad that had been sung ever since Dev's victory in Clare.

Until Lord French had the Sinn Fein leaders out of the way, he had not felt safe in issuing notice of his "voluntary" recruiting program. Eamon de Valera and Arthur Griffith would have ridiculed him out of Ireland.

Furious as they were, the Irish people had to smile over that "voluntary." Their military master told them they must raise fifty thousand recruits before October 1. After that date, he said, two to three thousand men a month would keep at full strength the Irish divisions already in the field.

Whatever the advantage Lord French might gain by the arrests, de Valera had been right about them influencing the coming election. It was held in East Cavan, in Ulster. Arthur Griffith won by twelve hundred votes.

Lord French must not have been listening when, in his Fourth of July speech, President Wilson said, "What we seek is the reign of law, *based upon the consent of the governed.*" For on that same July day the British banned Sinn Fein, the Irish Volunteers, and an Irish women's organization, declaring them dangerous associations whose meetings were henceforth illegal, and warning that anyone who called such a meeting or even attended it would be subject to arrest and prosecution.

With a sure instinct for the popular point of view, and a bland disregard for the truth, Lloyd George said in a July 5 speech: "President Wilson made it clear yesterday what we are fighting for!"

French's ban was extended to all public meetings, assemblies, or processions in Ireland, and he sent secret instructions to the police that the order applied also to sports, athletic contests, and any musical performances or open-air entertainment.

During the month of July 1918, police and soldiers armed with clubs or bayonets made eleven separate charges against those engaged in football and hurling matches, boating reunions, fetes, and concerts. But the Irish refused to be suppressed. On one August day, they played fifteen hundred hurling matches. On the fifteenth of that month, they held hundreds of public meetings. Of course, many of the speakers who addressed them were herded off to jail, and not only men, but women—a widow of a leader of the Rising was arrested along with one of Ireland's finest actresses, and the Countess Markievicz.

During September ninety-six Sinn Feiners were given prison sentences; in October, seventy-one more. The British were still appealing for Irish recruits, but getting few; they were plainly afraid to enforce the Irish draft. It was rumored that on October 15, the day Parliament was to convene, conscription would really begin. But by then, more than a hundred thousand Irish Volunteers were drilling and every one of them declared that he would resist with force if the English tried to take him.

The United States had been in the war for a year and a half, and by October 1918 over a million American soldiers were in France. Even if the Irish could have been persuaded to enlist, they were no longer needed. But the club of conscription was held over their heads as long as possible. When the war came to an end in November, the British had to think of something else to keep the Irish in order. They found it in the general election announced for early December.

Forty-seven of Sinn Fein's seventy-three candidates were in jail. Some of them managed to send out speeches, but these were promptly confiscated by the Post Office. De Valera's message was suppressed by the prison censors.

The Sinn Fein campaign manager was arrested and deported. James O'Mara, a wealthy Dublin manufacturer, took his place. The Sinn Fein manifesto he issued was heavily censored. The British tried to ban all Sinn Fein political meetings, and while many were held in spite of the ban, everyone knew that the whole election machinery would be under British control. And voters might correctly assume that if they voted for Sinn Fein, Ireland would be more heavily oppressed than ever.

Nevertheless, on December 14, Sinn Fein won every seat for which it had campaigned. And the British, who had been calling them ". . . a small bunch of rebels, supported by only a few fanatics," had to admit that Sinn Fein had swept the country.

Three days later the Irish Chief Secretary said ominously, "The Irish question will be settled, *peacefully or bloodily,* within six months."

But the Irish people were looking with optimism and hope at a ship plowing eastward across the Atlantic with President Wilson and his entourage, on their way to the Peace Conference in Paris. Before leaving New York, the President had received an appeal from more than a thousand New York Catholic priests to make the principle of self-determination apply to Ireland when peace terms were drawn up. At sea, he received a similar appeal from a great meeting held in Madison Square Garden.

If the President of the United States would only come to Ireland, and see for himself how matters stood! In Dublin, Eoin MacNeill called a public meeting which issued an invitation to President Wilson to visit the country.

In Lincoln Jail, Eamon de Valera was also thinking of the American President and how amazingly the influence of the United States had grown throughout the world. Perhaps Irish freedom would be determined not in London but in Washington. The American people must be made to realize that even as British leaders were prating of the "rights of small nations," England herself was allowing small Ireland no vestige of such rights.

Impatient, restless, burning with the desire to get into the fight again, Eamon de Valera made a wax impression of a prison key.

6

THE KEY
TO FREEDOM

IRISHMEN HELD in Lincoln Jail were getting much better treatment than they had received in other English prisons in 1916–1917. Except at night, their cell doors were left open and they might fraternize as much as they liked. Eamon de Valera was allowed to serve Mass and all the Catholics were frequent communicants. Their friends were allowed to send in food—but some of the prisoners chafed at the enforced inactivity and, with a couple of them, de Valera decided to try to escape.

One December day, he was studying two cartoons drawn by a prisoner on a card and addressed to the man's wife in Dublin. Everything that went in and out of Lincoln Jail was closely censored, but who could object to a Christmas card that showed the Irish getting the worst of it? One frame, labeled *Christmas, 1917,* showed a man, very drunk, trying to put an oversized key into the lock of his own house door and crying, "I can't get in!" The second, labeled *Christmas,*

1918, showed the same man in a jail cell, complaining, "I can't get out!"

Dev's shoulders shook with laughter. The pictured key was a replica of the one he had "borrowed" when the chaplain wasn't looking, and pressed into a piece of soft candle wax. Would the English suspect?

The card went through with no trouble by regular mail, but the prisoner's puzzled wife could make no sense out of it. To her, having a husband in jail was no laughing matter. She had, however, been instructed to pass on to Sinn Fein headquarters anything she received from her husband. When James O'Mara saw the card, he mused, "Let me think a minute—" then, "I believe I know why he sent it. Leave it here. Maybe you will be seeing your husband soon."

When she had gone, O'Mara showed the cartoon to Michael Collins.

"Lincoln Jail, is it?" said Collins with a grin. "I'll bet the Long Fellow is back of this. He must be getting tired of prison," and off he went to find a locksmith. The man quickly produced a key which matched exactly the picture on the card. Collins had it baked in a cake and saw to the icing himself.

The Irish prisoners waited and hoped. One day a guard brought some parcels which he said a quiet, soft-spoken gentleman had left for them. With the parcels was a beautiful cake, its artistic icing somewhat marred by several jagged thrusts of a knife where a suspicious warden had stabbed the cake through and through.

By the grace of God, he had missed the key! One of the men discovered it as he sliced the cake. With trembling fingers he brushed away the crumbs and tried the key in the lock of his cell door. It would not turn.

"It's too small," he reported sadly and the artist went back to work on a second card, this one with an intricate design and the words in Gaelic, "Key to Freedom."

The unsuspecting British delivered this card too, and a bit later let a second cake through to the Irish prisoners. The key concealed in it did not fit, either. But by this time Michael Collins and the debonair young Harry Boland had come over to England and they collaborated on a cake loaded with key blanks and files. With their aid, and that of a lock he had taken apart, a prisoner was able to make a master key. Somehow Michael Collins got a duplicate of it, and a time was agreed upon for Eamon de Valera and two others to attempt their escape.

They not only had to find their way out of the prison building, but through a double wall at the back. Beyond the door in the outer wall was an open field surrounded by a high fence. That field was a hazard, since the gate in its fence was directly across the road from a military hospital, and convalescing soldiers with their girls often strolled through and lingered near the gate.

On the night of February 3, 1919, Dev and his two companions waited for the appointed signal. Then, out in the darkness, Boland switched on his hand lamp. The prisoners answered with a flare that blazed up as one of them dropped the lighted match and set fire to the whole box.

Quickly they put out the flames. Dev swung back the door which had already been unlocked and stole out of the cell, the other two close behind. At each step they held their breath lest someone hear and sound an alarm. They were outside the prison, past the inner wall. Only the second wall stood between them and freedom.

And then they heard the scrape of metal on metal, a snap. . . .

"Dev—!" It was Michael Collins. "I've broken my key in the lock!"

Dev groped for the door, probed for the keyhole and gently thrust his own key in as far as it would go. He jiggled it. Something moved a bit. He pushed harder and suddenly the broken piece fell out on the other side. Dev's key went home in the lock. He turned it. The door swung silently out, and Collins' cold hand grasped his.

"This way," he whispered.

The five of them strode boldly across the field. As they neared the gate they heard voices.

"Good evening!" said Harry Boland cheerfully to the courting couples, brushed by them, and soon he and his companions were out of sight along the road.

Michael Collins was an adept plan maker. Those he had devised for this daring jailbreak worked without a flaw. The best men in British Intelligence combed the area. It seemed impossible for a prisoner as tall and distinctive in appearance as de Valera to vanish as he had. But Collins spirited him from place to place by car and train, finally leaving him with a friendly priest to wait until it was safe to go back to Ireland.

While he waited, de Valera caught up with what was happening in the world. He knew that President Wilson had come from America to take part in the Paris Peace Conference. He had heard something of Wilson's enthusiastic reception in Paris, in London and Italy. Everywhere people had hailed the American President for his democratic principles.

In Dublin, delegates elected the preceding December (except for those still in prison) had met at the first of the year to form an Irish Parliament, called in Gaelic, *Dail Eireann*. At its first meeting, three men were named to present Ireland's cause before the Peace Conference. Eamon de Valera had been one of those named. If he were only free to go!

Sinn Fein had published statistics that should have convinced anyone of British misrule in Ireland. Since the Rising, twenty-eight Irish citizens had been murdered. Six more had died of mistreatment in prison. The British constabulary and soldiers had made ninety-nine armed assaults on civilians, arrested five thousand, deported more than two thousand, and made sixty-six different proclamations against Irish liberty.

It would be impossible to hold the young men of Ireland in check much longer. Already they had killed two of the Royal Irish Constabulary in a raid for arms.

Discord, the devastating and destroying poison that had wrecked other Irish rebellions, was blessedly missing from this one. The Irish were standing together as one man.

"The fight for Irish freedom has passed into the hands of the young men of Ireland," said Limerick's Catholic bishop. "And when the young men of Ireland hit back at their oppressors, it is not for an old man like me to cry 'Foul!' "

The Irish Volunteers, now dignified by the new title, the Irish Republican Army, issued a bold ultimatum: "England has a choice. She can either get out of the country, or her foreign garrison will have to hold it in a perpetual state of war."

In the British Parliament, most of the seats assigned to the Irish delegation remained empty. And from an official of Dail Eireann in New York went a note to the American Secretary of State and to all foreign diplomats, telling them that the union of Ireland and England was at an end. What had happened after that official note was dispatched worried Eamon de Valera. He was strongly in favor of it, disturbed because two powerful Irish-American figures, John Devoy and Judge Daniel F. Cohalan, had refused to endorse it. The objections of Cohalan, a judge of the New York State Supreme Court, might be considered politically inspired. But John Devoy had been embroiled in every struggle for Irish freedom since the 1860s. It had been Devoy who arranged for the shipment of arms from Germany for the Rising. As editor of the *Gaelic American,* his was a voice that would be heard and heeded.

Something else worried him, too, Article X in President

Wilson's first draft of the League of Nations Charter. As it now stood, with Ireland registered as "an appendage of the British Crown," Article X might be interpreted in such a way as to keep her forever under British control.

A month passed with an impatient Dev still in hiding. Then suddenly the British released all the Irish prisoners. He was preparing to leave for Dublin when another difficulty arose. The Dubliners decided to give him a royal reception, complete with a presentation by the Lord Mayor of the keys to the city.

Dublin Castle banned that idea in a hurry and rushed fresh troops to the city to be sure the ban stood.

"Will he come, or won't he?" wondered the Irish, and some of them recalled what happened to Daniel O'Connell when the British banned a meeting of his. O'Connell submitted and that was the end of his influence in Ireland.

But Eamon de Valera met the challenge with his customary calm. "If we are to have trouble," he said, "let it be over something important," and went quietly home.

It did not lessen his popularity. In the first week of April he was elected president of Dail Eireann, and he immediately formed his Cabinet.

One of his first official acts was to issue a statement concerning that body of policemen, the R.I.C. For a long time they had been a highly respected and efficient peace-keeping organization. But now they were to all effects and purposes spies for the enemy, hence de Valera's merciless condemnation of them.

"The Irish people as an organized society have a right to defend themselves," wrote Dev. "These men of the R.I.C. must not be tolerated socially, as if they were clean healthy members of an organized life. They must be shown and made to feel how base and how vile is the position they occupy. To shun them, to refuse to talk or have any social intercourse with them or to treat them as equals, will give them vividly to understand how utterly the people of Ireland loathe both themselves and their calling, and may prevent young Irishmen from dishonoring both themselves and their country by entering that calling."

Dev's statement changed the image of the R.I.C. practically overnight. These men had always taken pride in their position. After the Rising, they had been forced into more and more official acts of repression which the majority of them did not condone, but they kept hoping things would change, that they could remain loyal to England and still love their own country. Dev's blast had a last-straw effect on the morale of the organization. Many resigned. Others who were about to resign were persuaded to stay—not by the English, but by Michael Collins, who thus vastly increased his number of spies in the ranks of the information-collecting R.I.C.

In the second session of the Dail, the able Collins had been named Minister of Finance and put in charge of a national loan. Since the British controlled all taxation and collection of revenues in Ireland, money had to be raised in other ways to support this new all-Irish Government. Collins advertised the loan. The British suppressed every newspaper that printed his advertisements. They made it illegal to buy Dail Eireann bonds, but the Irish bought them anyway.

In the United States, Irish-Americans pledged themselves to raise, within six months, a million-dollar Victory Fund for the Irish cause. Disturbing news concerning that fund now came to de Valera. Devoy and Cohalan, the same pair who had refused to endorse the notice of Irish independence, were saying that money from the Fund should be spent in the United States for Irish-American political purposes, such as opposition to the League of Nations. Dev was sure that people who subscribed to the Fund meant the money to go to Ireland where it was so desperately needed. Somehow this matter had to be settled and harmony restored in the ranks of the vitally important Irish sympathizers in America.

President Wilson, still in Paris, heard of growing political troubles at home. In the United States Senate, the Senior Henry Cabot Lodge made a bitter attack on the League of Nations. The President's secretary, Joseph Tumulty, cabled him that opposition to the League was growing more intense from day to day.

Wilson published a revised League Covenant, but no change had been made in Article X and others besides de Valera began to object to it. The Irish representative in Paris wrote to France's Georges Clemenceau, protesting that even the revised Covenant would maintain the *status quo* where Ireland was concerned.

Although news of it was not revealed until years later, early in April 1919, President Wilson suffered some sort of paralytic seizure. Either his doctor did not recognize it as such or he chose not to admit that he did. He cabled Tumulty that Wilson had come down with the influenza that was then of epidemic proportions in France and England. But the President's recovery was slow, and he became a different person after the attack—irritable, suspicious, far less able than before to cope with problems of any kind.

An especially aggravating problem for Mr. Wilson began to build with the arrival in Paris of an American Committee whose purpose was to obtain a hearing for Ireland at the Peace Conference. The Committee members were all highly respected figures in the United States and, recognizing their stature, Lloyd George promised to give them an interview. He could not see them immediately, he said, but he would definitely do so later—and in the meantime, they might visit Ireland.

A great cheering crowd greeted them in Dublin. Through someone's slip-up, they were even allowed to visit one of the prisons where, among other horror-provoking sights, they saw an Irish prisoner confined in an iron cage.

Eamon de Valera called a special session of Dail Eireann

to honor the American Committee. Afterward they were to go to a reception given by the Lord Mayor at the Mansion House, but at five o'clock that afternoon British soldiers turned out with machine guns and for two hours prevented everyone from getting anywhere near the Mayor's official residence. With de Valera, the American Committee watched the blockade from cars. Then, at seven o'clock, the soldiers suddenly evacuated their positions and permitted the reception to be held.

The Committee went on to tour Ireland, and on their return to Paris, Lloyd George discovered what a mistake he had made, for the three sat down and wrote a full report of the outrages being practiced by the British in Ireland and submitted it to the Peace Conference. The report concluded with the warning that if the Conference refused a hearing to the people of Ireland, it would have to share with Great Britain the guilt for "her monstrous crimes and atrocities, as well as for the bloody revolution which may follow."

Three days later the United States Senate, with but one dissenting vote, passed a resolution of sympathy with Ireland's hope for a government of her own choice and asked that Eamon de Valera, Arthur Griffith, and Count Plunkett be heard before the Peace Conference.

President Wilson was furious. When his secretary, Tumulty, cabled him from Washington to "do something for the Irish," the President berated the American Committee for its "extraordinary indiscretion" and told his secretary that British opinion was so inflamed that the situation was completely out of hand.

The persistent Tumulty came right back with another cable: "I hope you will not allow the indiscretions of the Committee to influence your judgment against Ireland. . . . In this country the Irish are united. . . . Could you not ask that Irish delegates be given a chance to present their case to the Conference?"

President Wilson was in a most embarrassing position. For years he had publicly declared that small nations should be allowed to determine their own governments. The Irish were not the only people who believed that the President meant what he said. The people of the United States believed it too, and they were shocked by his refusal to support Ireland's demand for self-determination. When the American Committee confronted him, he finally had to disclose the reason for his contradictory behavior. The Four Great Powers —Italy, France, England, and the United States—had agreed that no small nation could appear before the Peace Conference *without unanimous consent of the four.* Of course, there was absolutely no chance that England would permit the rebellious Irish to be heard.

The news was a blow to Irish hopes everywhere, but it came as no surprise to de Valera, nor would he permit it to discourage him. Whether or not the American President did anything to help Ireland, there was still a strong pro-Irish sentiment in the United States. And Dev could see American power and influence increasing in the world with every passing day.

That was why, two weeks earlier, he had disappeared from Dublin.

"The President of Dail Eireann has gone to Paris," rumor had it. "He will make one last plea to the Peace Conference. . . ."

Of course the English had not given him permission to go anywhere; in fact their "G" men were searching frantically for him when, on the seventeenth of June, Arthur Griffith announced cryptically:

"By and with the advice of the Ministry, the President has gone on a mission abroad."

"Self-government for the Irish people . . . is a right and a necessity."

New York Evening Post—*June 1919*

7

LAND OF THE FREE

ONE NIGHT ABOUT a week after the Griffith announcement a lanky figure in seaman's clothes strode ashore from a ship that had docked that day from England. It was Eamon de Valera, and waiting for him in the shadows were Harry Boland and an official representative of Dail Eireann in America, Dr. McCartan.

"Where are your clothes?" Harry gripped his hand.

"The rats gnawed holes in them," said Dev. "Anyway, if the 'G' men are looking for me, isn't this a good disguise?"

"No one will bother you here," said Dr. McCartan, but Dev was not so sure of that.

He had been in hiding all the way across the Atlantic and was cramped and sore from lack of exercise. And for one accustomed to the chilly fresh breeze of an Irish summer, the muggy heat of this New York June night was like a steamy blanket pressing down on him until he found it hard to take a deep breath.

The others located a suit of ready-made clothes and took him to Rochester for a few days with his mother. It was hot here too, but there were trees and shade, and he could walk the kinks out of his legs. Then he was off to Philadelphia to hear Joseph McGarrity's side of the Irish-American controversy.

He was still there when the American Committee's report of British atrocities in Ireland was published in full by the New York *Herald*. At once the Irish problem grew hotter than the sticky asphalt of Philadelphia streets.

The British ignored the report at first. Then the British Secretary for Ireland denied that there was any truth in it. But a few days later, one of Sinn Fein's political rivals corroborated every word, calling the report "the first really true and comprehensive picture of the present British rule in Ireland."

The world was still wondering what had happened to de Valera when, on June 23, Harry Boland sent the reporters racing for telephones by telling them that the "President of Ireland," Eamon de Valera, would appear at New York's Waldorf-Astoria that afternoon at five o'clock.

Dev got a noisy reception. A crowd of several hundred waited outside the hotel, waving the Irish tricolor and singing Irish songs. As the police rushed the tall man through, an old Irishwoman darted past them, grabbed Dev, and gave him a resounding kiss.

His ready-made suit had been replaced by a well-tailored dark gray one and with it he wore a white silk shirt and a plain blue silk scarf. When he objected to such finery, Harry Boland said seriously, "You have no choice, Dev. You are here in this country as president of an independent nation. You will just have to dress the part."

"But I am not President of Ireland," Dev protested. "There is no such office—"

"If you try to explain the difference between the president

of the Dail and the president of the country, you'll just confuse people." Harry grinned.

"Well, all right," said Dev reluctantly, "but I wonder what Arthur Griffith will think when he sees the lofty position to which I've been elevated!"

The clothes were not only richer and finer than any he had ever worn, they also seemed hotter. New York had had a heavy thunderstorm a couple of days before Dev's official introduction to the city, and the humid heat built up afterward until it was worse than it had been in the Dartmoor workroom.

As reporters swarmed 'round him, however, de Valera forgot everything but Ireland. He delighted them by saying, "It is to the press rather than to diplomats that we, the common people, must look if we are to save democracy."

And when an inquisitive reporter wanted to know how he got out of Ireland, the man's colleagues laughed with de Valera as he replied in his faint brogue, "Mr. Boland here advised me to say that I was the first man to come across the Atlantic by air—but I won't."

"Are you an American citizen?" asked another.

Again a smile warmed Dev's face. "That's a good question. I was born in New York. But I am an Irish citizen."

"Did you forswear American citizenship?"

"I did not," he replied." I lost it automatically when I enrolled as a soldier of the Irish Republic."

A Chicago reporter called him "This tall, smooth-faced, clear-eyed young Irishman," and wrote glowingly about how de Valera had compared Ireland's battle for freedom to that of America in 1776.

A few days later the same Chicago paper printed their reporter's description of de Valera: "He is not the 'typical' Irishman. He has the bronzed face of the Spaniard, the deep passionate brown eyes of his father's people . . . he is tall, very tall, and inclined to thinness for a man of his giant bone structure . . . he was a noted athlete in his younger days."

And then the reporter tried to clear up the misunderstanding that was being fostered by British propaganda, which made it appear that Sinn Fein and "southern Ireland" were all Roman Catholic, and that was why the "outnumbered Protestants of Ulster" refused to be "ruled in Dublin."

"De Valera is a Catholic," wrote the Chicago newsman, "but many of his associates are of the Ulster Protestant persuasion. He makes no distinction between men as to creed. All he asks is that an Irishman love Ireland with all his heart."

The day after de Valera's official arrival, President Wilson, still in Paris, received a long cable from his secretary in New York:

"We must have a policy in regard to Ireland which we can explain to the American people," it ran. "At present Ireland threatens to reopen all the rifts which comradeship in the war was closing."

Tumulty quoted the New York papers which were promoting self-government for Ireland and concluded, "Frankly, this represents the opinion of the average man in America, without regard to race or religion. The arrival of de Valera in New York is going to intensify the feeling and the Republicans will take advantage of it." (President Wilson, of course, was a Democrat.)

Enthusiastic as it had been, the New York reception for Eamon de Valera was mild compared to the frenzy in Boston when crowds welcomed the "Irish President."

But pro-Irish sentiment was burgeoning in New York as well. A week after the Boston visit, Eamon de Valera was escorted by veterans of the Fighting 69th from his "White House" in the Waldorf to Madison Square Garden, where a crowd applauded for ten minutes before Chairman Judge

Cohalan could quiet them sufficiently to make himself heard.

De Valera's plea was for Irish freedom—"freedom from the rule of bayonet, from rifles, from machine guns, freedom from police spies and perjurers, from the invasion of our homes without writ or warrant, freedom from murder by British government agents, freedom from invented crimes and imprisonments without trial—and not least, let us have freedom from the infamous libel spread by the organized official propaganda of the British Government!"

Perhaps he was not yet a great orator, but as he spoke the passion in Dev's voice brought those fifteen thousand people to their feet again and again, shouting so that it hurt the ears.

"Whatever one thinks of de Valera and his cause, he cannot be lightly dismissed," warned the New York *Times*. "He is stirring feeling in the United States that will have to be reckoned with. . . ."

The next great American city he visited was Chicago, where his train was met by a crowd of ten thousand. And at a luncheon given him by the mayor, six brawny guests picked Dev out of his chair before he could speak, hoisted him to their shoulders, and paraded him around the banquet hall.

De Valera headed back to New York, his spirits revived by the exuberant Chicagoans. He needed encouragement, for not only had the Irish in Paris been finally rejected by the Peace Conference, but Judge Cohalan and John Devoy were calling completely impracticable Dev's five-million-dollar bond drive for Ireland.

"Their noses are out of joint," said a friend wisely to de Valera. "Until you came, *they* were the spokesmen for Ireland."

"But I am under instructions given me by the Dail," Dev protested. "And I have every intention of carrying them out."

"Cohalan isn't used to being defied," warned his friend, "and John Devoy is old and deaf and crotchety. He will do just about whatever Cohalan recommends."

It was all too clear that de Valera's dream of uniting the Irish-American leaders had been a visionary one. The divisions among them were too deep and too old. Through the years many an Irish visitor had deplored their angry bickering. But de Valera was sure that Cohalan and Devoy did not truly represent the many thousands of Irish-Americans. It was to them he would make his appeal. At home Dail Eireann showed its faith in his judgment by setting the goal of the bond drive at ten million dollars rather than five.

The situation in New York was unpleasant enough, but de Valera was more gravely concerned by the political picture in Washington, D.C. President Wilson, back at last from Paris, had made a speech to the Senate insisting that the League of Nations Covenant be ratified without changing a single word. And Article X was still part of that Covenant. So far, the senators were stubbornly maintaining that changes must be made. It was reported to de Valera that they controlled enough votes to block ratification. But President Wilson was about to begin a long swing around the United States. A strong sentiment in favor of the League of Nations was growing among the American people. And at every stop on his tour, the President would appeal to them to bring pressure on the Senate, to bring the country into the League.

Eamon de Valera was making plans for a tour of his own. Americans must hear both sides of this story, he believed, must be informed that Article X of the League Covenant could keep the Irish forever under British rule.

On September 3, people close to the American President were concerned about him as he left Washington. His schedule for the next month would have exhausted a man much younger and in better health than he. Temperatures all along the way would be in the nineties, with dizzying waves of heat shimmering about the rear platform of the train where he must stand to make many short speeches.

President Wilson had never entirely recovered from the

seizure suffered in Paris. It had probably influenced his judgment more than anyone realized. Certainly this nation-wide tour was ill-advised. On September 25 news flashed from Colorado that the President had collapsed and was being rushed back to Washington.

A week later, Eamon de Valera boarded a train heading west. He was glad to leave New York. As the "Irish President," he had to live in a luxurious hotel, wear fine clothes, be feted at innumerable banquets and receptions. There was seldom a chance to be alone and he craved solitude, as he craved a bracing country hike.

For a man of his height, a long train trip was a trial. Sleeping berths were too short, seats too confining. But he was fascinated by the landscape unrolling past his window. He had always wanted to visit the American West. Two weeks out of New York found him there, in the company of some native Americans.

"Squatting on the ground in a chilly clearing of a rugged northern Wisconsin forest, Eamon de Valera, President of the Irish Republic, became Chief and a member of the Chippewa tribe," wrote a Milwaukee reporter. "He was tired from an all-night train trip, but he took a spirited part in the ceremony, even to smoking the pipe of peace!"

It was an experience Dev would never forget. The Indians gave him a beaded tobacco pouch, a coral necklace, a pair of moccasins. When they bestowed on him the name of their chief who had signed a treaty granting them their reservation, de Valera said with deep feeling, "I hope that I may yet sign the treaty which will give *my* people their lands, and freedom with it!"

He took a boyish delight in the backwoods dinner that followed. Venison, duck, prairie fowl—all were delicious. He climbed back on the train with fresh vigor. This made up for all the strait-jacketed formality he had been enduring.

There were longer and longer periods between cities where

he must stop to make speeches. The train steamed west across Minnesota, across the Dakotas, into the wide, empty reaches of Montana. Dev wondered if this were the route Vivion de Valera had taken years before. He wished he knew more about this father he could not even remember. Then the first faraway misty-blue peaks of the Rockies began to appear in the west, looking so unreal one could not say whether they were clouds or mountains. Black smoke rolled past the windows as the train labored up the long grade and presently Dev could see the white mantle of an early snowfall on the taller peaks. How Sinead would love all this! And wouldn't the children enjoy getting out on horseback, like the youngsters he saw whooping and yelling as they raced their mounts away from a lonely schoolhouse. . . . Ah, this was better than the cities!

Then down the western slope of the mountains across the panhandle of Idaho he went, to the state of Washington, and more crowds, more speeches. Before his party reached Portland, Oregon, they found the West even wilder than they had heard it was, for in nearby Centralia what the papers called "Red sympathizers" fired into a parade and killed four members of the American Legion, whereupon one of the killers was promptly lynched by a mob.

In Portland a war veteran, influenced perhaps by British propaganda, tore the Irish flag from de Valera's car. But Dev spoke that night to a crowd that filled the auditorium and found them an attentive and appreciative audience.

Here he and his companions snatched another day of freedom; he walked the rest of them to exhaustion along the rough paths of the Columbia River Gorge, insisting on viewing every waterfall that curtained the steep, rocky walls.

In Portland they were joined by an old friend, James O'Mara, one of the three trustees named by Dail Eireann to be responsible for money collected in the bond drive. O'Mara brought distressing news from Ireland. Raids, arrests, torture, and imprisonment were once again the order of British business. But Irish opposition was more stubborn, more efficient than ever. Britain's Royal Irish Constabulary was gradually being driven out of the smaller towns and villages; their barracks were being burned—almost five hundred by this October 1919. As he and O'Mara traveled southward to California, Dev knew the old grief, but also a new pride in the Irish people.

With all this fresh in his mind, Eamon de Valera made one of the best speeches of his tour in San Francisco. There were many homesick Irish in this westernmost American city, many more who might not think of Ireland as home but still loved her. They were quick to see the injustice of Article X. No one here wanted the United States to enforce a Covenant that would keep Ireland in chains, and they'd be telling their senators that!

At last back in New York, with O'Mara in charge of the bond drive, de Valera could devote his entire time to propaganda for Irish freedom. He was puzzled by some of the things that had happened recently. The United States Senate continued to refuse to ratify the League Covenant, and that was gratifying. But was it not strange that President Wilson's message to Congress on the second of December made no mention of it? Why had the President refused to receive the British Ambassador, who had been waiting for some time to present his credentials? Could it be Wilson's health? Not a word could be obtained from the White House concerning it.

In January 1920, a general election was called in England and Ireland. Although the British contended, as always, that most of the Irish people did not support their own government, the election proved the opposite. Eleven of Ireland's twelve boroughs declared themselves in favor of an independent Irish Republic. Most significantly, even in Belfast, the twelfth borough, the Irish Republic gained support, and in all Ulster those who wished to remain with England took only twenty-two towns, the Irish Republicans twenty-three.

De Valera read the election results with a grateful heart. No longer could the English say that Ulster did not want to remain part of Ireland. No longer could they pretend that the present Irish leaders were backed by only a few of their people. Perhaps England would now take a fresh view of Ireland, would decide that the Irish were able, after all, to govern themselves!

The next day he knew the folly of placing any confidence whatever in the English, for their troops in Ireland only redoubled their oppressive tactics. January saw a thousand raids, 220 arrests. February was even worse, with four times that number of raids.

It was just as well that all the tragedy in Ireland was not reported in the United States. Eamon de Valera had enough to worry about right here in New York. For presuming to tell them that money collected for Ireland should be sent to Ireland, Judge Cohalan and John Devoy had resolved to get this upstart of an Irish "President" out of the way. Too many people donating to various Irish Relief collections had begun to agree with him.

Using the pretext of a speech in which de Valera compared Ireland's position with that of Cuba, John Devoy launched a vitriolic attack on him in the Irish newspaper which Devoy controlled. Then he and Cohalan invited seventy-five of their supporters to an anti-de Valera meeting on March 19. To make sure Dev would not be around to defend himself, they had an invitation sent him for a banquet in Chicago on the same night—a banquet that did not exist.

Unfortunately for the two plotters, Joseph McGarrity, de Valera's friend from Philadelphia, appeared at their meeting and after hearing Cohalan accuse de Valera of ignorance of American politics, refusal to take advice from his betters, trying to make Ireland an ally of England, being arrogant and a money-waster, McGarrity jumped to his feet and demanded that Dev be given a chance to reply to the charges.

"He's in Chicago," said Judge Cohalan smugly.

"He is not," said McGarrity. "He's at the Waldorf and I insist that he be brought here."

"No one is to leave this room," said the chairman. But McGarrity persisted, "Then telephone to him—and get him over here!"

Within a few minutes, de Valera and Harry Boland were at the door. One of Cohalan's henchmen tried to bar their entrance, but Boland picked him up bodily and set him aside. Then the two walked down the aisle to the platform.

As if he were appearing for the first time before these people, Eamon de Valera patiently explained to them that he was responsible to the government of Ireland and to her people. He had been careful, he said, not to interfere with American affairs, but with anger roughening his deep voice he accused Cohalan and Devoy of being hostile to him and his work.

"I know that this meeting was called for the purpose of driving me back to Ireland," he said.

"No! No!" cried some of his listeners.

"Will you believe me if I produce a letter which shows the conspiracy against me was going on as long as six months ago?" he demanded.

"Who wrote the letter?" asked a man in the front row.

"It was John Devoy," answered Harry Boland.

"That's a lie!" yelled Devoy, who sometimes was not as stone-deaf as he appeared to be.

De Valera turned to McGarrity. "Produce the letter."

But there was so much tumult the letter was never read. Cohalan finally apologized to de Valera. Dev accepted his apology and shook hands with him. A Catholic bishop pleaded for peace and asked everyone there to kneel down and pray!

It was not peace, however, but a truce, soon broken. When the American political conventions were held that summer, Cohalan and Devoy fought every attempt de Valera made to get a plank for Irish freedom into Republican and Democratic platforms. As a result, neither platform so much as mentioned Ireland, and the two schemers blamed de Valera for it.

Arthur Griffith was later to declare that Eamon de Valera had accomplished extraordinary work in America, but for years to come Dev's conflict with the two self-appointed Irish-American leaders would be quoted by every enemy as "de Valera's failure in the United States."

Nevertheless, it was partly due to his influence that the Senate ratified the European Peace Treaty which officially ended World War I with the remarkable reservation that their country must "adhere to the principle of self-determination and the resolution of sympathy with the expectations of the Irish people for a government of their own choice . . ." and after further ponderous federal language, they recommended Ireland's membership in the League of Nations.

Dev sent a cable to Arthur Griffith concluding with a jubilant "Ireland has been given her place among the nations by the greatest nation of them all!"

The year and a half that Eamon de Valera spent in the United States was wearisome, trying, exhilarating, and discouraging by turns. During the summer of 1920, Sinead was able to join him for a few months, and as always her presence made the worst trials bearable. Even the humid heat did not seem so hateful as it had before she came.

He dreaded her departure, all the more because of the increased fury of the British in Ireland. In addition to oppression by regular British army units and the R.I.C., the Irish were now suffering from depredations of the Black and Tans, thus nicknamed because they had been hastily recruited and wore makeshift uniforms of those two colors.

That autumn the mayor of Cork was murdered as he opened his own front door. Terence MacSwiney took his place, was arrested, went on hunger strike, and for seventy-six days the world watched him die rather than submit to his oppressors.

In October Sinead de Valera went back to Ireland. Her husband felt he must stay in America until after the November election. President Wilson was not running, but Dev felt that the election of Wilson's Democratic successor would be interpreted as a vote of confidence for the League of Nations, whose Covenant had still not been ratified by the American Senate.

It seemed that no sooner was one crisis past than a worse one sprang up in its place. By an overwhelming vote, Americans elected a Republican President, Warren G. Harding. But later in November the newspapers were full of stories about "Bloody Sunday" in Dublin and the "unarmed British officers" who they said were shot down by the Irish, some in the presence of their wives. Naturally de Valera was asked for an explanation, but he had no idea what had actually happened.

There was an appalling lack of communication between those inside Ireland and the outside world. News reports of Irish events were almost invariably written by the British.

De Valera yearned to get home. Many Irish leaders there were held captive. Some had been assassinated. In December word came that Arthur Griffith was in prison again and Eamon de Valera set the machinery in motion for his return.

He went back the way he had come, secretly, a political stowaway hidden deep in a ship by loyal Irish seamen. And although the English set a closer watch for him than ever, he evaded them. Michael Collins met him and on Christmas Eve the two walked together into Dublin.

"Hatred plays the same part in government as acids in chemistry. And here in Ireland were hatreds which, in Mr. Kipling's phrase, would 'eat the live steel from a rifle butt.'"
    Winston Churchill—1921

8

THE TERROR

EVEN ON Christmas Eve, Eamon de Valera could not go to his home. Everyone there was well, he learned from Michael Collins, who had risked arrest himself again and again by insisting that he take the small Sinn Fein stipend to Mrs. de Valera and, time permitting, have a romp with the boys. Reports from him of those personal "inspections" had eased Dev's anxiety about his family during his stay in the United States. But the night of his arrival in Dublin Dev must have felt this continued separation from Sinead and the children almost more than a man should be called upon to bear.

He was glad, however, that his family lived some distance from the heart of Dublin, where Collins had found a house for him. James O'Mara's daughter, Patricia, describes vividly what the city was like that winter of 1920–1921:

"I dropped off to sleep my first night at home," she writes, "and woke again quaking with fear. Fusillades seemed to sweep through the room, from the roof above me, from the roofs opposite, up and down the street the crackling of rifle shots broke the unnatural silence of curfew. I woke my sisters. I thought it was a battle. I thought it would be safer if we went downstairs where there were shutters. They laughed at me. Every night, they said, the snipers were on the roofs annoying the British patrols. I'd get accustomed to it. . . ."

Soldiers in lorries did more than patrol the streets and shoot back at rooftop snipers. After the hour of curfew, only British military forces were allowed out, so it was a fine period for them to raid houses, hotels, and even convents, in search of men "on the run," as the Irish phrase so accurately described Irish patriots trying to evade the British.

A clever Sinn Fein carpenter had concealed a closet in a wall where Dev might hide, should the British decide to search this particular house. A few nights after his arrival, people were routed out of every building in a whole city block not far distant, and it was evident the object of that search was Eamon de Valera.

To make sure the hunt for him would be carried out with the greatest possible enthusiasm, Britain's Irish Secretary reviled de Valera as "a man with a fancy for ditch murders" and said that he belonged to "a race of treacherous murderers." There was no man the British would have liked better to take into custody, unless it was the efficient and elusive Michael Collins, who, with Cathal Brugha, was directing the entire Irish resistance movement.

Dev soon discovered how valid had been his concern over the dearth of accurate Irish news in America. Rioting British forces had burned the city of Cork and swaggered afterward through Dublin streets with bits of charred cork defiantly displayed in their hats. Yet British leaders boldly stated that it was the Irish themselves who set fire to the city, and this was the "official" version of the holocaust.

"They call us 'gunmen,' and 'the murder gang,'" said Collins grimly, "but look at this . . ." and he handed Dev an *Irish Bulletin* with statistics for 1920. During the year, forces of the British Crown in Ireland had wantonly murdered 203 men, women, and children, none of them in any armed conflict.

The *Bulletin,* secretly published by men of the Irish Republican Army, was being sent every day to foreign news correspondents. Without it, the world would have only England's side of the story, which told only of murders *by* the Irish.

That reminded de Valera of the "Bloody Sunday" murders of British officers by the Irish, represented to him in New York as "cold-blooded assassinations of military men who were only doing their duty."

Michael Collins said heatedly, "They were spies—every last one of them, planted here to murder Irish leaders. They tortured prisoners—killed innocent men—I had no more feeling for them than I would have for a deadly snake. . . ."

"Were you absolutely sure?" asked de Valera.

"Sure! Cathal Brugha was the one who sifted the information—you know how rigid Cathal is, and how cautious—he eliminated a couple of names, because he thought we weren't absolutely 100-per-cent sure of them."

De Valera nodded. He knew that Cathal Brugha was scrupulously fair.

And the murders by the British that same Sunday afternoon in Dublin's Croke Park had been scarcely mentioned in American newspapers. Yet, as Collins told him now, the Black and Tans had driven up in lorries and opened fire over the fence into a crowd of more than seven thousand people watching a football match. They killed a dozen spectators, wounded perhaps sixty. . . .

"They continued to fire for ten minutes," said Michael Collins bitterly, "with everyone running this way and that, frantically trying to escape. You can imagine how many were trampled and hurt in such a stampede—do you mean to tell me this wasn't even reported in America?"

"They didn't make much of it," said Dev.

"Things are going to change," Collins assured him. "In fact they already have changed. Erskine Childers is doing a great job on his articles, and every one of them is being published in England."

As Dev knew, Erskine Childers was the Anglo-Irish owner of the yacht which had brought the shipment of guns and ammunition to the Irish Volunteers at Howth six years before. Childers had gone on to fight for England during the war, but now he had come over wholeheartedly to the Irish cause. And his articles kept pounding away at the British position in Ireland, the savagery of the Black and Tans, the wanton destructiveness of another recently organized British military group, the Auxiliaries.

Now, in January 1921 the English people themselves were taking a good look at what their government was doing in Ireland. They did not like what they saw. Even the British General Nevil Macready admitted that the Black and Tans were a tough lot. Some of them had been released from jails to go and fight in Ireland. A good many, at some time or other, had been in prison.

As for the Auxiliaries, most of them were recruited among unemployed veterans of World War I. They had caused so much trouble for Brigadier General Frank P. Crozier, their commanding officer, that by the preceding November he had had to get rid of fifty of them for various infractions of discipline.

A month and a half after de Valera's return to Ireland, in the little village of Trim, thirty of Crozier's Auxiliaries stood by while Protestant shopkeepers were being robbed. He dismissed twenty-six of them, held five for trial. But suddenly his orders were countermanded from England. General Crozier resigned. Promptly, nineteen of the men he had dismissed were restored to duty. Two of the five awaiting trial went out and robbed a bank. When someone asked why they were not shut up while awaiting trial, Britain's Irish Secretary explained that there was no place to put them, so many Auxiliaries were already under close arrest.

"What is now being done in Ireland is exactly what we condemned the Germans for in Belgium," said England's Archbishop of Canterbury. "When the Germans perpetrated cruelties in Belgium, it was said that the German *people* could not be blamed, but the reply was that *the German people acquiesced.* Exactly the same charge can be brought against the British *people* if they acquiesce without protest in what is being done in Ireland today."

Still in hiding, Eamon de Valera wrote a letter and sent a copy of it to each member of the British House of Commons. It pointed out their personal responsibility for the war in Ireland. But when the House assembled, Prime Minister Lloyd George soothed them by his bland statement that he was satisfied with the progress of the Irish war! John Redmond's son, Captain William Redmond, one of the few remaining Irishmen who still sat in the British Parliament instead of Dail Eireann, then asked the Prime Minister for an inquiry into the Irish situation, but he was refused.

While the Dublin Brigade of Collins' I.R.A. continued to attack British forces in the capital, out in the country the I.R.A. fought as Americans had fought in Revolutionary War days, hiding behind trees and hedges, picking off the enemy one by one. For this the British *Weekly Summary* called them "black-hearted assassins."

It was time to put the matter straight, and Eamon de Valera did so in an interview. Throughout the struggle with the British, de Valera and other Irish rebel leaders had found they could trust newspapermen not to reveal places of rendezvous and to repeat accurately what they were told. Dev said that the I.R.A. was the Irish Republican Army, a national military body under the control of Ireland's legally elected Dail Eireann. The government was back of, and fully responsible for every action of that army.

"What about ambushing British forces?" asked the reporter.

De Valera rose to his full height. "The British forces are in our country as invaders," he said bluntly, ". . . waging upon us not only an unjust but a barbarous war. Protected by the most modern war-appliances, they swoop down upon us and kill and burn and outrage . . . why should it be wrong for us to do our utmost to see that they will not do these things with impunity?"

Brown eyes intent on his listener, he pressed his point: "If they may use their tanks and steel-armored cars, why should we hesitate to use the cover of stone walls and ditches? Why should the element of surprise be denied to us?"

The reporter, of course, had no logical answer for those questions. And a few days later, de Valera went into the situation even further:

"If German forces had landed in England during the recent war, would it have been held wrong for Englishmen to surprise them?" he demanded. "Wrong to harass the invader by every means in their power? If it is not wrong for Englishmen, why wrong for us?"

His statements were published in full, and how men of the Irish Army cheered when they read them! He had made it clear that England waged war on all Ireland, not merely on "the small band of extremists" to which Lloyd George was fond of referring.

The Prime Minister was doing his best to hide from the English people what was really happening in Ireland. He said that the Sinn Fein patrols, military, and police had all vanished, that he had the Sinn Fein murder gang "by the throat." But another British general gave him the lie, saying that in

Ireland law and order had given place to bloody, brutal anarchy.

"England," he wrote, "has departed further from her own standards, and further from the standards even of any nation in the world, not excepting the Turk and Zulu, than has ever been known in history before."

The general's letter was written in March, and on the sixth of that month, in Limerick, the Crown forces proved him right about their savagery. During the hours of curfew, there was a knock on Mayor Michael O'Callaghan's front door. His wife opened it. Two men, revolvers in their hands, pushed past her and shot her husband dead. Later that night armed men forced their way into the house of a former Limerick mayor, George Clancy. His wife struggled with them and was shot through the arm. Her husband was killed.

Ever since the murder of one mayor in Cork and the arrest of another, officials of every city in Ireland had wondered if the British aim was not to destroy every Irish leader. In Limerick it had been arranged that should something happen to O'Callaghan, James O'Mara's brother Stephen would take over as mayor. The O'Maras took the precaution of installing a steel door at the top of the stairs, in case the murderers in Limerick tried to increase their score to three.

Eamon de Valera wrote to James O'Mara, still working for Ireland in New York: "Despite the crushing pressure that the British are bringing to bear, the people are standing up wonderfully, and I think the worst is past. . . ."

But one evening a week after de Valera had written that letter, a friend found him in the house, leaning over a table, head in hands.

"Have you a headache?" asked the friend.

"No, a heartache," said Dev.

That had been a day of public mourning in Dublin, for the British had hanged six Irish prisoners.

How much longer, how much more could the Irish people endure?

A talented Irishman wrote that he would rather see his country a "blackened rock in the ocean" than see her surrender to her brutal assailants. But Eamon de Valera remembered that Cromwellian savagery had once brought Ireland to her knees. How similar was this present campaign of British terrorism—the burning of countless homes, destruction of hundreds of cooperative creameries and places of business. The British had arrested thousands of heads of families, destroyed food supplies. Areas under martial law were refused any compensation for property demolished by forces of the Crown. Even hospitals could get no support.

Ireland would have had to give up before now, de Valera felt, if it had not been for the help given by relief organizations in the United States and even in England. For months the American Committee for Irish Relief had been sending shiploads of food and clothing to Ireland. In London, a committee of American delegates opened an office to supervise the distribution of their "White Cross Fund." In northeast Ireland, where the frightful struggle had been further embittered by a pogrom, or organized massacre, against the Catholics, the Americans aided thousands of Catholic workers who had been driven out of Belfast.

The British were furious. They seized collecting boxes, raided White Cross offices and the homes of White Cross workers, but they dared not suppress the Fund. American sentiment was too strong. British Ministers preparing to go to America to represent their government at the Washington Disarmament Conference were gravely disturbed when they discovered that the White Cross Fund was supported throughout the United States, and by the most eminent of American citizens.

Eamon de Valera began to note some results from the pressure of American pro-Irish sentiment on England. A series of messengers began to arrive in Dublin, each with a different plan to "settle the Irish problem." De Valera would see none of them. He did not believe in secret deals. If Lloyd George wanted peace in Ireland, let him declare a truce!

For more than a year Lloyd George had been plotting to entangle the Irish in a web from which they would find it impossible to escape. They wanted a Republic, that they had made very clear. They could not have a Republic. If Lloyd George's government even considered such a mad solution to the Irish problem, it would find itself the next moment embroiled in a worse fight with the stubborn British Ascendancy of Belfast.

Six counties around that northeastern Irish city must remain in the British Empire. The other twenty-six counties could not go it alone economically, for Belfast was really Ireland's only manufacturing center. Eventually England would have the whole country again securely under her control.

This was the reasoning behind Lloyd George's cynically named "Better Government of Ireland Act." He had shepherded it through the British Parliament, and although it had never been ratified by any Irish body, it had become law during the preceding December, just before de Valera arrived home from New York.

The Act provided for two separate legislatures in Ireland, one for the Six Counties in Belfast, the other for the rest of Ireland in Dublin. And the elections set for May 1921 were for members of two legislatures, not one.

Sinn Fein Republicans all over Ireland declared they would vote, but only for the Irish Parliament in Dublin, Dail Eireann. Sinn Feiners around Belfast, most of them Catholic, were hindered by the British in every way possible. They voted at the risk of bodily assault. Sinn Fein organizers were dragged from polling booths and beaten. Long before the election, thousands of Catholics had been expelled from Ulster. But in spite of all the English and the Ascendency could do, twelve Sinn Fein Republicans in the Six Counties were elected to Dail Eireann.

For the English that was twelve too many. On June 8 a renewed anti-Catholic pogrom began with the double murder of two young men by Ulster Specials. During the following week five Catholic men were assassinated by the Specials, and a sixth was beaten to death. Then eleven more were shot dead, and 150 Catholic families were driven from their homes.

In the rest of Ireland every Sinn Fein Republican had been returned to Dail Eireann and everyone in England and Ireland recognized that an overwhelming majority of people wished an independent Republic. Only a few—Winston Churchill was one—saw that England had gained a great tactical victory with the establishment in Belfast of a separate Parliament, which was, of course, under British control.

"From that moment," wrote Churchill, "the position of Ulster [i.e., the Six Counties] became unassailable."

The Irish nation was not yet subdued, but England had succeeded in dividing it.

Lloyd George had to do more than this about the Irish problem, however. Even in his own Wales, people were protesting loudly about his management of the Irish war, and criticism mounted daily in England and the United States.

In Ireland, the British general commanding regular military forces recommended that martial law be extended to all Ireland, that all means of transportation be seized, that civil courts and newspapers be suppressed. But even as he proposed the plan, he admitted that if things were not settled by October, England would have to send over a fresh army. The I.R.A. might have only three thousand men to England's eighty thousand, but many British military men were cracking under the strain of guerrilla warfare in Ireland.

So many bombs had been lobbed into lorries cruising through the Dublin streets that wire mesh had to be stretched over them. Dubliners promptly dubbed them "birdcages," and an old flower-seller at the corner of St. Stephen's Green gibed at the British one day:

"The Boers put you in khaki, the Germans put steel helmets on you, and now the Irish have put you in cages!"

Sir Henry Wilson, himself Irish-born but with a virulent hatred for the country, wanted the English to "sweep up all motors, bicycles and horses, close Post Offices and banks, and then *drive* . . ." the same sort of drive carried out by Cromwell perhaps, when he put to the sword every living creature in Drogheda and Wexford and sent the Irish fleeing to the stony fields of the west with his ultimatum "To Hell or Connacht!"

Winston Churchill estimated the cost of such a campaign in men and equipment at a hundred thousand new troops and police, thousands of armed cars, and cordons of blockhouses and barbed wire throughout southern Ireland. Even with that equipment, Churchill warned, the British would have to search and question every individual in Ireland to have hopes of success.

With two other British government leaders, Austen Chamberlain and Lord Birkenhead, Churchill suggested that the English threaten to use the most drastic means of control in Ireland, and at the same time offer a large measure of self-government. Lloyd George agreed to reinforce troops in Ireland to the fullest possible extent and if, by July 12, the southern Parliament were not in operation in accord with the Better Government of Ireland Act, threatened the country with martial law in the south.

The day after this decision was reached in London, 120 Irish soldiers destroyed the Dublin Customs House, the center of nine British Administration departments. It was a thorough operation. Next morning only the walls were standing. The English had lost every record of local government and the files of two great departments of taxation.

Then the I.R.A. announced that henceforth, if the English destroyed Irish Republican property, the Irish would burn the houses of the British Ascendancy who were known to be giving active aid to the enemy.

Lord Birkenhead shook his head and prophesied that the struggle would continue for a long time. But a month later, King George V went to Belfast to speak at the opening of the northern Parliament. He pleaded for an end to the strife in Ireland, appealed to all Irishmen to forgive and forget. He said he had an earnest desire that a Parliament might soon be set up in southern Ireland. And Lloyd George, Winston Churchill, Sir Henry Wilson, Lord Birkenhead, Austen Chamberlain, and all the other British government leaders who had been laying intricate plans for a stepped-up campaign of oppression in Ireland found their campaign scuttled.

"No British Government in modern times," fumed Winston Churchill, "has ever appeared to make so sudden and complete a reversal of policy."

But as the King was speaking in Belfast, a company of troops raided a house in Blackrock, just outside Dublin, and found a small group of men sitting in the garden. One of them was clearly wearing a disguise. When they left, they took him along. And at the prison, they discovered that they had the man they had sought so long and had not even recognized.

President de Valera was, once again, in jail.

"It was time for a little intrigue."
  Peace by Ordeal—*Frank Pakenham*

9

DIVIDE AND
CONQUER

EAMON DE VALERA prepared himself for interrogation, for more endless hours in a prison cell, for everything except what happened to him the morning after his arrest.

A polite British official came in.

"You are free to go home," he said, and within moments Dev found himself being driven in a private car along the road to Greystones.

Sinead could not believe he was actually home again. She too had braced herself against all the horrors, known and unknown, that his arrest might bring.

"What happened?" she asked, after she'd made sure he was safe and sound.

"I don't know." His brown eyes were puzzled. He could not understand the British change of heart and he did not trust it. Were they trying to bribe him with his own freedom to give up the struggle for freedom of his country?

He picked up the *Freeman's Journal* and read the speech

King George had made the day before in Belfast. "End to strife in Ireland . . . earnest desire for a southern Parliament . . ." Those were fine words, but would the British Government heed them? De Valera would wait and see. Michael Collins said the British were making plans for a tremendous onslaught against the Irish in July. Was that to be canceled? Had England a conscience after all?

The King's speech really had been a straw in the wind. The day after Dev's release a letter came to him from Prime Minister Lloyd George, inviting him and anyone he might select to a conference in London. This was what Dev had been waiting for. Now that the thing was out in the open, he could accept the invitation gladly. But he used great care in his reply. If the talks were to succeed, he insisted, the British must recognize that Ireland was one country, not two, and had a right to decide for herself how she should be governed.

Lloyd George refused to accept such provisions and a series of letters went back and forth between London and Dublin, with both men jockeying for position.

On July 4, in honor of the American holiday, the Stars and Stripes flew in front of the Mansion House in Dublin. Inside the Lord Mayor's official residence, Eamon de Valera was talking to men of the Unionist minority, who would prefer to remain under English rule, as well as to the Sinn Fein majority, who wanted nothing but an independent Republic. Eoin MacNeill was there. So was Arthur Griffith, looking thin and pale after months in Dublin's Mountjoy Jail. The British Ascendancy leader in Belfast, Sir James Craig, had been invited to come but had declined.

Terms for a truce with the British were discussed, and de Valera made it clear that the Irish would not surrender their arms, as Lloyd George had been insisting they must.

A day or so later Lloyd George conceded this most vitally

important point. On July 9, 1921, the truce was announced and it came into force on the eleventh.

That day there were bonfires on the hills. British military forces were kept in their barracks. The fighting men of the I.R.A. came home to music and dancing, although some of them said harshly that it was not yet time to celebrate. Like de Valera, they had no reason to trust the British. Nevertheless they took advantage of the truce to bring home the bodies of their comrades who had been hurriedly buried during the years of war.

Eamon de Valera took five men with him to London. They were Arthur Griffith, Austin Stack, Count Plunkett, Robert Barton, and Barton's cousin Erskine Childers, the writer whose pen had told the Irish story so poignantly and so well during the last two years.

Before they left Dublin, de Valera issued a proclamation which showed how little he expected to accomplish by the coming talks.

"Should force be resumed against our nation, you must be ready once more to resist," he cautioned.

Few heeded him. They'd won, hadn't they? Hadn't they forced the British to ask for a settlement?

De Valera had reason to be pessimistic. A few days before, General Smuts, from the Union of South Africa, had come secretly to Dublin. And all he would talk about was the great advantage to be gained by coming into the British Empire. A Republic would not give the Irish as many benefits, he insisted or any more independence. Arthur Griffith and de Valera had listened and said little themselves. After these years of bloody war, of bitter reprisals, of arson, torture, and murder, would any Irishman be willing to swear allegiance to the British Crown? From Dev's viewpoint, there was only one solution to the Irish problem, and that lay in complete separation from England.

But if Eamon de Valera had one outstanding trait, it was the ability to look at both sides of a question. He could see how Lloyd George would naturally think of Ireland as part of England, and be convinced that a free, independent Ireland would be a threat to England. How could she be otherwise, of course, after seven hundred years of British misgovernment?

On July 12, in his official residence, No. 10 Downing Street, Lloyd George received Eamon de Valera in a setting carefully arranged to impress him. The Prime Minister ushered Dev into the room where the British Cabinet met. An Imperial Conference had been in session here and with an expressive wave of his hand at the comfortable chairs about the big table, Lloyd George said:

"There sits Canada, there South Africa . . ." He named them in turn, pausing at what he indicated was a vacant chair, then hurrying past, only to return to it a little later. As de Valera still made no comment, Lloyd George said with some irritation, "One chair remains vacant . . . waiting for Ireland. . . ."

De Valera maintained his silence. He had not missed the significance of the chair, or of the great world map extending across the wall, liberally splashed with red to show the possessions of the far-flung British Empire.

Lloyd George found it impossible to negotiate with de Valera. "It is like sitting on a merry-go-round and trying to catch the swing in front," he complained that night.

At their third meeting they were as far apart as ever. Impatiently, Lloyd George said, "When we meet for the fourth and last time, I will let you have our terms in writing."

De Valera shook his head. "I must see them in advance."

After much argument and protest, it was agreed that de Valera would receive the terms late on the night of July 20. They were not as acceptable as he had thought they might be. They offered Ireland Dominion status, but it was not even equal to that enjoyed by Canada and other members of the Commonwealth. There were a number of qualifications—the British still in possession of certain Irish harbors, for instance, and Partition, with Sir James Craig in control of the Six Counties split off from the rest of Ireland by Lloyd George's Better Government of Ireland Act.

"I could never agree to such terms," de Valera told the Prime Minister the next morning. "I cannot even carry them back officially to Ireland, so I am returning them to you."

Lloyd George's blue eyes blazed fire. "Do you realize that this means war? Do you realize that the responsibility for it will rest on your shoulders, and yours alone?"

Dev looked coolly down at him. "No, Mr. Lloyd George," he said, "If you insist on attacking us it is you, not I, who will be responsible."

"I will publish these terms immediately for the Irish people to see," threatened Lloyd George.

"Go ahead," said Dev. "But I thought nothing was to be published unless both of us agreed."

"That was a little matter." The Prime Minister tossed back his shock of white hair. "We are dealing with big things now."

"So I must assume that is how you keep your promises," said Dev. "Have your way. You publish your terms and I will publish my refusal of them."

He turned to go.

"Won't you give me a considered answer?" asked Lloyd George in a sudden change of tone.

"Certainly, if you give me time to consult my colleagues."

"Very well," said Lloyd George.

Nothing was published. The de Valera party went back to Dublin to lay the British terms for a treaty before the Cabinet. Before leaving London, Arthur Griffith told Austin Stack he thought the British terms were pretty good. In Dublin, Michael Collins and the Army Chief of Staff, Rich-

ard Mulcahy, joined Griffith in expressing approval of them
—except, of course, for Partition with those Six Counties
remaining under British rule. Cathal Brugha and Austin
Stack, however, were horrified that any Irishman would even
think of making peace on such terms.

When it came to a vote, however, Griffith, Collins, and
Mulcahy went along with Brugha and Stack. The Cabinet
unanimously rejected the British terms. And about two
weeks later that rejection was confirmed by Dail Eireann
without one dissenting vote.

Then began another exchange of letters, with de Valera
asking the British Prime Minister why England had any right
to restrict Ireland's independence, and Lloyd George pointing out in reply how fully the present British terms would
have satisfied the demands of any Irish leader of the past.

Finally, a Treaty Conference was arranged with the British. To the dismay of many and the despair of some, Eamon
de Valera refused to be a delegate. Remembering President
Wilson's failure at the Paris Peace Conference, he felt that,
if he remained in Dublin, the British would not be able to
force any hasty decisions on the Irish delegation. They could
always say that terms must be submitted to their President
and the Cabinet before they could be accepted.

Arthur Griffith consented to head the Irish delegation. To
the very last, Michael Collins protested against going. The
English had put a fancy price on his head and only a keenly
developed sixth sense and an alert guardian angel had kept
him alive up to now. Should the conference fail and the war
be renewed, he wouldn't last long once the "G" men got a
good look at him. But de Valera felt the Irish must have a
delegate with Collins' boldness and courage, and finally persuaded him to go. Over Arthur Griffith's objections, de Valera
insisted that Erskine Childers act as secretary to the delegation.

Gavan Duffy, who had defended Sir Roger Casement five years before; Eamon Duggan, another lawyer; and Robert Barton were also named.

October 11, when they arrived in London, was hot and dry, as the long summer had been. The strange weather was affecting tempers everywhere. And even without the heat, the Irish might well have been uneasy. They faced a formidable team of negotiators. Lloyd George, the "man who won the war," was the wiliest diplomat in the Empire; Winston Churchill, Secretary of State for the Colonies, had a command of the English language few men boasted; Austen Chamberlain, Leader of the House of Commons, was one of a family which had been in British politics for generations; Lord Birkenhead, the brilliant lawyer who had prosecuted Casement, was one of the stanchest supporters of the British Ascendancy in Belfast; Sir Hamar Greenwood, Britain's Irish Secretary through the years of the Terror, and blamed by Ireland for the excesses of the Black and Tans, had also been fighting to keep northeast Ireland under British control. There were two more Englishmen at the Conference, of lesser importance but considerable ability.

By comparison, few of the Irish delegates had ever been heard of before in England. The British were prepared to find Arthur Griffith a man of intelligence, but they expected Michael Collins to be the dark, sinister figure painted by their propaganda department as "head of a murder gang." They were quite taken aback by the twinkle in Collins' blue eyes and the way his whole body shook when he laughed. Lloyd George's secretary wrote appreciatively of Collins' handsome features, his forehead "crowned with a thick crop of dark brown hair."

They would have indeed been surprised to know that Collins' mind was a tidy filing cabinet. He forgot no small detail; he neglected nothing; he knew far more than anyone in the

Conference what was happening all over Ireland—the pogroms in Belfast as well as the drilling of the I.R.A. in the
rest of the country.

The Irish had agreed to keep to themselves, to accept no
English hospitality, lest they be influenced by it. Invitations
from the Irish-born painter Sir John Lavery and his beautiful
wife were, however, accepted by all of them save Childers.
And since the Laverys entertained Irish and British alike, the
opposing delegations became better acquainted than they
could possibly have done at the conference table.

After the first few sessions attended by the entire delegations, Lloyd George decided that Arthur Griffith and Michael
Collins might discuss matters more freely if the others were
not present. As leaders of the Irish delegation, it would be
perfectly proper, he said, for them to meet the British leaders.
So private sessions began and after one such meeting at Winston Churchill's home, Lloyd George reported with a pleased
smile on his round, pink face that he and Arthur Griffith had
really made progress. And Michael Collins became the firm
friend of Lord Birkenhead.

During the course of the Treaty Conference, the delegates
kept in close touch with de Valera. Griffith sent frequent letters. And Collins was always showing up in Dublin for a
weekend, not only to confer with the President, but to talk
to members of the secret Irish Republican Brotherhood and
keep in close touch with the I.R.A.

De Valera had never underestimated the difficulties faced
by the delegates. But as Collins, a man of action, fretted over
the passing days and Griffith grew weary of submitting the
same demands and seeing them rejected, de Valera welcomed
the long-drawn-out sessions, feeling that time was on the side
of Ireland.

On November 16, more than a month after the Conference began, proposals for a treaty with Ireland were
drafted by the British and duly presented to de Valera and

the Cabinet in Dublin. A week went by. Then the Irish sent Lloyd George a memorandum for changes in his treaty draft. The Irish still insisted on indepedence, on equality with England in the League of Nations, on an Irish Army and Navy, and an undivided Ireland. But they yielded to the British on what seemed highly important points.

If the British would agree to the Irish provisions, Ireland would accept the British Crown as "head of their association," would agree with the British Dominions on matters of common concern, would give no other nation control over Irish territory. When de Valera added to these concessions a promise to consider British naval claims on Irish ports for five years and a recommendation for Irish trade agreements with the British Dominions, he thought he had conceded a great deal.

In the opinion of Brugha, Stack, and Countess Markievicz, he was conceding far more than he should. Arthur Griffith, although he continued to hold firm against British demands, clearly felt that there was no chance to get them to agree with the Irish terms, that de Valera was asking the delegates to go on fighting a losing battle.

On November 29 a new element was injected into the parleys. From Belfast, Sir James Craig announced that the "rights of Ulster" were to be in no way sacrificed or compromised. Lloyd George must have promised him secretly that Partition of Ireland was to continue, for Craig spoke further of his "unflinching determination not to go into an all-Ireland Parliament."

Three days later, the entire Irish delegation came home to Dublin with what Lloyd George said was a final draft of the treaty, containing absolutely the utmost concessions the British could make.

It was Arthur Griffith's first trip home since the beginning of the Conference, and de Valera was at once aware of the influence the British had brought to bear on him. He was dour and discouraged. Both he and Michael Collins urged the Cabinet to accept the British terms.

They were very much like the ones Lloyd George had handed to de Valera the previous July—those which Dail Eireann had rejected. Ireland, they said, must become a British Dominion, the Irish must take an oath of allegiance to the British Crown. Belfast and the Six Counties were to remain separate unless they chose to come into an all-Ireland Parliament, and Craig had demonstrated how slight the chance was of that happening.

"This is a document I cannot accept," said de Valera flatly.

Glaring at Griffith and Collins, Cathal Brugha inquired, "Who was responsible for the splitting of the delegation, so that two members did most of the work and the others were not kept fully informed?"

"The British Government was responsible for the arrangement," said Griffith stiffly, "but it had the approval of the whole delegation."

"Yes," said Brugha, "they selected their men, did the British!"

Griffith objected. De Valera mediated. Brugha withdrew the remark and said later, "I did not mean to cast any reflection on the honor of these men, but before they were selected at all, I told them what I thought of their ideas of freedom."

The debate continued. De Valera said he could not subscribe to the Oath of Allegiance, nor sign any document that would give the Six Counties power to vote themselves out of the Irish State.

"I can understand you giving up independence for national unity," he said to Arthur Griffith, "but you have got neither this nor that."

But Dev believed the delegates had done their best and he told them so. He would like to see them go back and secure peace, but they must tell the British that the proposals had to be amended. If they were not, the Irish would take the consequences, war or no war.

Griffith would not listen to any suggestion of renewing the war. But after hours of argument, Cathal Brugha said to him, "Don't you realize that if you sign this thing, you will split Ireland from top to bottom?"

Griffith stared at him. "I suppose that's so," he said slowly. "I'll tell you what I'll do. I'll go back to London. I'll not sign that document—" but he went on to say that if the British refused to negotiate further, he would "bring it back and submit it to the Dail, and, if necessary, to the people."

Up to that point, de Valera had almost decided to go to London with the delegation, to add his influence to theirs. Griffith's promise eased his mind. And now the whole delegation agreed to reject the Oath of Allegiance as written, and, if a break must be made with the British, to make it on the question of Irish unity. Even Brugha and Stack agreed that it would be worthwhile to compromise a little, if Ireland could be united once more.

With the delegates on their way again, Dev left for the west of Ireland, reviewing troops everywhere he went, speaking to the people, warning them against too easy optimism. In Limerick on Monday, December 5, he said grimly, "We are not bluffing. Nothing will be accepted that deprives the nation of the essentials of freedom. Our resistance may not be sufficient to drive the English out of Ireland, but it will be sufficient to prevent them ruling Ireland. This is a separate nation, and never to the end of time will they get from this nation allegiance to their rulers!"

The people of Limerick who had lived under the worst of British military oppression, had seen their mayor murdered, their finest men taken off to concentration camps without trial, their businesses destroyed, had every reason to fear renewal of the war. But they accepted de Valera's judgment.

"Contests like this," he said, "go in the end to spiritual forces, even though it takes a long time."

Dev stayed that night with the O'Mara family, his mind so constantly on the struggle going on in London that it was hard for him to think of anything else. Suppose a treaty were signed, would the British keep it? The "Treaty Stone" here in Limerick, where Sarsfield had signed for Ireland, was a lasting reminder of treaties the British had violated.

He remembered the Indians in America's Wisconsin forest, priding themselves on the liberty and independence they had wrested from a powerful government. But it was not in the nature of powerful governments to honor treaties with weak, ineffectual, and dependent peoples. Even the United States had broken faith, time and again, with every one of her Indian tribes. Eamon de Valera could see clearly that the only way to negotiate was through strength and stubborn, unyielding adherence to principle.

Because he was a man of principle, he expected others to be. He was not alarmed, only puzzled, when word came that night that the treaty had been signed. The British must have been bluffing to a far greater extent than he had thought, to give in so suddenly. Strange, though, that someone in the delegation had not informed the President before releasing the news.

He was to preside the following night at a Dante Centenary celebration, to be held in the Mansion House in Dublin. During the long ride across the central plain of Ireland, he grew increasingly uneasy.

And when he strode into the Lord Mayor's room, and found Cathal Brugha and Austin Stack awaiting him, one look at their faces confirmed the fears that had been growing in him all day.

"What news?" he asked tensely.

"Bad." Stack handed him a newspaper which had, that

evening, published an outline of treaty provisions which de Valera had not been permitted to see.

His face white, Dev read them through. Without a word he donned his university gown and walked toward the door. On the other side, a crowd awaited him. As his hand touched the knob, Eamon Duggan hurried in with an envelope.

"What is this?" asked de Valera.

"The Agreement," said Duggan. "It is to be published in London and Dublin at the same time, eight o'clock."

Somewhere a clock chimed eight.

"Do you mean," asked Dev incredulously, "that this is to be published whether I have seen it or not? Whether I approve of it or not?"

Duggan's face flushed dark red and he could not meet Dev's eyes. "Well," he said lamely, "that is what was arranged."

De Valera thrust the envelope under his robe and stalked into the next room. The door closed behind him. Duggan, Brugha, and Stack heard a burst of applause. It is doubtful that Eamon de Valera heard it, or anything that followed after he had, with stony face, introduced the speakers.

The celebration of the Dante Centenary must have seemed a hundred years long to the Irish head of state who sat there with sorrow for Ireland wringing his heart, broken promises torturing his mind. Faithlessness by the English would not have surprised him. But he had put his whole trust in the loyalty and courage of Arthur Griffith and Michael Collins. How could Griffith go back on his pledged word? How could the whole delegation disregard—not the person of Eamon de Valera, but the dignity of the office of the President of Sinn Fein and the Irish Republic?

The next day a grim-faced de Valera held a conference with Cabinet members Brugha, Stack, and William Cosgrave. Dev called the man who had charge of publicity and told him to summon the absent delegates by telegram, to consider the circumstances under which they had signed the agreement in London.

The man raised his eyebrows. "This message reads as if you were opposed to the settlement, Mr. President."

"That is how I intend it to be read," said de Valera.

Next day the Irish delegates appeared, together with Stack and Brugha. Try as he might, de Valera could get no answers to the questions that had been hammering at his brain since he heard they had signed the treaty. *Why* had they surrendered so precipitously? *Why* had they not granted their President the smallest of courtesies he surely was entitled to expect from them? Could they not have called to say they had signed before releasing the news to the whole world?

The meeting lasted for seven hours. The more de Valera pressed the delegates, the more stubbornly they defended themselves. And at the end, he had to give up and call for a vote. Griffith, Collins, Barton, and Cosgrave proposed to submit the Treaty to the Dail. Stack and Brugha voted with de Valera against such action.

De Valera accepted the majority decision. He summoned the Dail to consider the Treaty. But he said to the Irish:

"A great test of our people has come. Let us face it worthily, without bitterness, and above all, without recrimination. There is a definite constitutional way of resolving our differences."

It was a reassuring message, far more so than Dev's next public statement.

"In Ireland there is a proverb which says, 'In a
quarrel, whoever comes out safe, or does not come out
safe, the man between never comes out safe.' "
    Sean O'Faolain

10

THE MAN

BETWEEN

PROCLAMATION OF THE PRESIDENT OF IRELAND, DECEMBER 7,
1921.

You have seen in the public press the text of the proposed
Treaty with Great Britain. The terms of the Agreement are in
violent conflict with the wishes of the majority of the nation as
expressed freely in successive elections during the last three years.
I feel it my duty to inform you immediately that I cannot recommend the acceptance of the Treaty, either to Dail Eireann or the
country. . . .

They were puzzled people who read de Valera's proclamation. Every newspaper in the world was trumpeting the joyful
news that peace had come to Ireland. The Catholic bishops
had declared themselves in favor of the Treaty. Dreading
further trouble with the British, Irish businessmen were for
its immediate ratification. Why would Ireland's President re-

fuse to accept it? Why had he called a special session of the Dail? Had the Irish delegates been tricked into some kind of British trap? Griffith and Collins insisted that they had brought back an honorable settlement. Who was right?

De Valera had always liked and admired Arthur Griffith. The admiration had, apparently, been mutual. Griffith had stepped aside so that de Valera might become Sinn Fein's first president. He often spoke in glowing terms of de Valera's ability and character. During periods when Griffith might well have resented the honors given this newcomer to the political scene, he had shown no sign of jealousy.

However, P. S. O'Hegarty, one of Griffith's strongest supporters, wrote of him: "He believes intensely in himself, and he has no real faith in anybody else. . . . Once he has made up his mind on anything he never changes. In controversy he is like a bulldog; he is always the last to let go and by that time there isn't much left of the other man's case. As a controversialist he is able and totally unscrupulous, but he is nearly always right."

This was the man who now opposed de Valera in the Dail. Immediately after signing the Treaty, Griffith had sent a telegram to the United States claiming victory for Ireland. He was not about to retreat a step from that claim. He would not even admit that he had signed the Treaty under threat of "immediate and terrible war," although Robert Barton and Gavan Duffy testified that it was such a threat which made them sign.

Robert Barton gave the most emotional speech of the whole debate in the Dail. He confessed that his signature to the Treaty had broken his oath to the Irish Republic, an oath that was, to him, the most sacred bond on earth. He went on to describe how just before the signing of the Treaty, the Conference had broken down and how, the following day, Arthur Griffith, Michael Collins, and he once again met the English negotiators.

Barton defended Arthur Griffith, saying that he had sought repeatedly to have the terms of the Treaty referred back to Ireland. He told how Lloyd George had denied that request, declaring that the delegates themselves must either accept or reject.

"The English Prime Minister," said Barton, "with all the solemnity and power of conviction that he alone, of all men I met, can impart by word and gesture—the vehicles by which the mind of one man oppresses and impresses the mind of another—declared that the signature and recommendation of every member of our delegation was necessary or war would follow immediately!"

Afterward, said Barton, at their headquarters, Arthur Griffith, Michael Collins, and Eamon Duggan were for acceptance and peace; Gavan Duffy and Barton were for refusal— war or no war.

"For myself, I preferred war," cried Barton. "I told my colleagues so, but for the nation, without consultation, I dared not accept that responsibility. . . . I signed—and now I have fulfilled my undertaking. I recommend to you the Treaty I signed in London!"

So, in spite of Griffith's denials, the Irish delegates had somehow been hypnotized by the little Welsh Prime Minister. Years later, Lloyd George's secretary, Geoffrey Shakespeare, was to write: "I have never . . . understood why the Irish accepted the ultimatum at its face value. Why did they not call the bluff?

"Supposing Arthur Griffith had said, 'Are you really going to break the truce and plunge Ireland again into war without giving the Irish Cabinet the chance even of discussing your latest proposals?' How could Lloyd George have persisted with the ultimatum if Arthur Griffith had argued like this?"

The Prime Minister's secretary asked himself curiously if Arthur Griffith might not have signed the Treaty because he thought it would then be more difficult for the Dail to repudiate it.

But, Shakespeare concluded, the simplest explanation was probably the true one. "Lloyd George threatened war, he looked war, and he intended war, unless they signed. No one could doubt his sincerity when his words 'imparted conviction,' his eyes flashed lightning. How dare t.ey question the ultimatum? They were awed and they signed."

No Irishman would have been willing to admit he was awed. Arthur Griffith denied it to the end. Neither would he admit that the wily Lloyd George had tricked him in any way. Griffith seemed honestly to believe that he was right. His support of the Irish Republic had always been somewhat reluctant. He felt now that, together with the personal assurances given him by Lloyd George, the Treaty provisions were as good as the Irish could ever get. A reinforcement to his stubborn stand was his ever-growing dislike for Erskine Childers, who, from the first and to the very end, had opposed signing of the Treaty. In the Dail, Griffith sat with a black look on his face when Childers rose to speak.

Erskine Childers, like Arthur Griffith, had a logical mind, one which could analyze and compare. He was the only man who apparently could touch a quivering, painful nerve in Griffith—perhaps remind him of things he refused to think of—and for that reason he became a hated adversary.

Childers pointed out that the Treaty did not give Ireland Dominion status, as had been claimed. The British troops might be withdrawn tomorrow, but they could return whenever England was pleased to announce that there were strained relations with a foreign power, or when she was actually at war with a foreign power.

And it was not only Childers who disproved the claims being made for the Treaty by its Irish supporters. In the English Parliament, Lloyd George was making it quite clear what a triumph he had won over the Irish:

"The Treaty imposes on Ireland a limitation on the raising of armaments and the training of armed men," boasted the Prime Minister. "The first thing we provided for was free access to all the Irish harbors and creeks, in case of war. In wartime one cannot wait for discussions between governments as to where you can send your ships, or land your men."

The longer Lloyd George talked, the less independent Ireland was shown to be. Yet when Griffith spoke to the Dail, he said, "We have brought back the flag; we have brought back the evacuation of Ireland after seven hundred years by British troops . . ." and he went on to declare that the Treaty gave Ireland equality with England.

Kevin O'Higgins, speaking in favor of the Treaty, maintained that it gave Ireland complete control over her internal affairs, made her liable to no taxation from England, allowed her to maintain an army and defend her coasts—a statement that was, that very day, being contradicted by Lloyd George in the British Parliament.

Eamon de Valera noted everything that was being said in that Parliament. He was convinced that Arthur Griffith and Michael Collins had been hoodwinked.

"I am against this Treaty," avowed de Valera, "not because I am a man of war, but because I am a man of peace; I am against this Treaty because it will not end the centuries of conflict between the two nations of Great Britain and Ireland. . . ."

And Austin Stack declared that even if the Treaty gave Ireland all the freedom and independence boasted by Canada, he still would not accept it. How could any Irishman accept membership in the British Empire? How could he take an oath to be loyal to the English King? "Was it for this," demanded Stack, "that our fathers have suffered . . . for this our comrades have died on the field and in the barrack yard?"

Even more bitter arguments came from the women members of the Dail. One black-clad widow of a hero of the Easter Rising, who had herself spent many miserable months in British jails, called the Treaty a surrender of all Ireland's national ideals.

"If it is ratified the result will be a divided people," she warned. "The same old division will go on; those who will enter the British Empire and those who will not, and so England's game of divide and conquer goes on."

During the weeks of argument and discussion in the Dail, it became evident to the thoughtful observer that a powerful force was being exerted in favor of the Treaty. It was the secret organization to which Eamon de Valera had belonged, briefly, before the 1916 Rising, and resigned from because he did not believe such an organization had any place in a Republic. The Irish Republican Brotherhood was bringing a powerful influence to bear on all its members. Michael Collins was one of its leaders.

It was still hard for de Valera to believe that the courageous Collins had signed the Treaty. When he rose to speak, Dev strained his ears to catch every word, every telltale inflection.

"I say that rejection of the Treaty is a declaration of war." Michael Collins tossed back the dark hair from his forehead and repeated the phrase, "Rejection of the Treaty means your policy is war. If you do this, if you go on that as a national policy, I, for one, am satisfied. . . . I signed it because I would not be one of those to commit the people to war, without the Irish people committing themselves to war."

Had the vote been taken that day, many thought it would have gone against the Treaty. But Michael Collins moved that the Dail adjourn until January 3, and so it did.

Ever since de Valera's proclamation against acceptance of the Treaty, there had been increasing efforts by pro-Treaty deputies and by the press to discredit him and his leadership. Before debate began on the Treaty in Dail Eireann, he had called a secret session of the Dail and presented to it a rough draft containing suggestions for a new Treaty agreement. In it he had attempted a far more difficult task than bringing together the idealistic Brugha and Stack with the practical Collins and Griffith; Dev had tried also to devise a plan which would bring in Sir James Craig and his Protestant supporters in the North, as well as one the British Cabinet might accept.

When he presented this rough draft for consideration, de Valera had asked the members of the Dail to consider it only as a working agreement, and to keep it to themselves, since he did not feel it was ready to be seen by the public in its present form. Neither did he want the British to see it until it had been revised by the Dail itself. He had no reason to suspect that any member would violate his confidence.

As the debate sessions wore on, de Valera had continued to work on the rough draft, and by the time the Dail reassembled in January, he had formulated a series of proposals which he felt most of the members might support. This revised version he called "Document No. 2," and he intended to present it as an amendment to a motion approving the Treaty, but he was thwarted by his opponents and decided to withdraw the whole document, at least for the present.

Divisions were widening almost hourly in the ranks of the Irish leaders. Nevertheless de Valera was taken quite off guard on January 5 by an attack made on him in the *Freeman's Journal* which even his opponents called "infamous." The attack was greeted that afternoon in the Dail by a chorus of disapproval, but Arthur Griffith did not join with the rest.

"The press has a right to say whatever it likes," he said in his cold, level voice, and de Valera knew at last that here was an enemy.

It was Griffith who gave to reporters the confidential, rough draft which de Valera had presented to the Dail in that secret session of a few weeks before. It appeared in the press on January 5, side by side with de Valera's "Document No. 2," under headings which seemed, as one Irish historian wrote, "diabolically conceived to confuse and prejudice everyone who read them."

Immediately, in an impassioned speech, Eamon de Valera offered his resignation to the Dail. The *Irish Independent* quoted him in full, and added, "If there was one to doubt the sincerity, the transparent honesty of the Irish leader, that doubt would pass with one glance at the man as he stood before his colleagues."

But Griffith and Collins called his resignation a trick.

The very unfairness of the accusation hurt Dev cruelly. If the Dail were faced with trickery, it was not by himself. He consented to withdraw his resignation, but only if Griffith would consent to a vote on the Treaty within twenty-four hours.

Irish historian Dorothy MacArdle tells how it was on the morning of January 7, 1922, when Arthur Griffith rose to move approval of the Treaty:

There was silent, brooding anxiety throughout Ireland. There could be no doubt that the thought of losing de Valera's leadership dismayed those who, since 1916, had elected and re-elected him, with complete unanimity, to the leadership of Sinn Fein, of the Volunteers, of Dail Eireann, of the whole national struggle. Some whose dread of consequence had withheld them from opposing the Treaty were tempted to vote against it rather than lose his guidance at such a time. This fact was recognized and resented by Griffith's adherents now.

Griffith, on the other hand, had done much to lessen de Valera's influence by his misrepresentation of "Document No. 2." Men who would have voted against the Treaty if they had believed the alternative to be a firm stand for the Republic were led into supporting it, believing now that the alternative was merely the offer of another compromise and one which the British might refuse.

Cathal Brugha made one last speech which should have cleared up their doubts. He was devoted to the Republic, opposed to the Treaty, yet he could support de Valera's compromise which the Dail had refused even to discuss.

Griffith glowered as Brugha turned with an impassioned reminder of how Griffith had stepped down in favor of de Valera in 1917, and begged him to do as much for the country now.

"I tell him," Brugha cried to the Dail, "that if he does this his name will live forever in Ireland!"

Griffith's response was a lengthy speech in favor of the Treaty and defense of his action in signing it. It was not a final settlement, he declared. "It does not forever bind us not to ask for any more . . . in the meantime we can move on in comfort and peace to the ultimate goal."

Michael Collins had never had any intention of keeping a Treaty that had been "signed at the point of a gun." From his point of view, it would get the British soldiers out of Ireland. Then, as other Dominions had gained more freedom and independence with each year, so, Collins believed, would Ireland. Neither he nor Griffith was the man of conscientious principle that de Valera was. But each had done the best, as he saw it, for Ireland.

"What would have happened," wrote a de Valera partisan later, "if Michael Collins and Arthur Griffith had come back to Ireland in secret, had said to the president, 'Dev, we signed this Treaty with a gun at our heads. It isn't what we wanted, but it's the best we can get right now. Help us to work it out, will you?' "

"Would Eamon de Valera have turned his back on them? Would he have announced to the country that he was against what they had done? This will forever be one of the most tantalizing questions in Irish history, and there is no use in asking it, because neither man asked de Valera's help. Instead they tried to cram the Treaty down his throat. They went around him to the people, representing the Treaty as something it was not, representing his ideas as something they were not. They split the Irish leadership. They split the people."

That the Dail was split had long been apparent, but the lines of division were still fluid. In the vote that followed Arthur Griffith's speech on January 7, 1922, no one knew whether a deputy answering the roll would answer "For" or "Against." The foreign correspondents who jammed the galleries could not even tell which was which, for the proceedings were in Gaelic, and their untrained ears could not distinguish a vote against the Treaty from one in favor of it. At last an Irish newspaperman took pity on them and helped them keep the tally. It was close, first to one side, then to the other, and not until the very last was anyone sure what would come out of this desperately important struggle. The final count showed only seven more in favor of the Treaty than against it.

Numb with the shock of what he had thought could never happen, President de Valera got slowly to his feet. "The Republic goes on," he said in a flat, unemotional tone, "until the people have disestablished it." Then, "We have had four glorious years of magnificent discipline in our organization. The world is looking at us now. . . ."

A bitter gorge rose in his throat. He sat down and buried his face in his hands to hide his tears. England had truly conquered them at last. For they were bitterly, completely, and finally divided. And the man to whom that mattered most deeply, who had tried hardest to keep it from happening, was to bear the greatest blame for the division.

"If there are to be struggles . . . and if blood is to be shed,
then in the first place it ought to be Irish blood. . . ."
Lord Birkenhead's Speech to the
House of Lords—June 1922

11

WALL OF GLASS

AFTER THE TREATY vote in Dail Eireann, Eamon de Valera
resigned the presidency and Arthur Griffith was elected in
his place. In a regretful moment, Griffith said of his predeces-
sor, "There is scarcely a man I have met in my life that I have
more love and respect for. We want him with us." And de
Valera had reacted strongly to a suggestion from a deputy
that there would be war between brothers.

"That is all nonsense," he said quietly. "We have a nation
that knows how to conduct itself."

A month later, he might not have been willing to repeat
that statement. The Griffith forces had the most overwhelming advantage which any political party can gain over any
other—control of the press. Newspapers in Ireland and England were almost 100 per cent pro-Treaty and anti-de Valera.
Phrase by phrase they began to erase from the minds of the
Irish people the image of the man who had led them, united
them, counseled them wisely for the last four years. Suddenly
he was pictured as a quibbler, an extremist, a wild-eyed im-

practical fellow whose only desire was to plunge his country once again into war.

There was no effective way to fight the flood of obloquy. De Valera tried his best with an unwearying series of speeches throughout the country, only to find his words quoted out of context, their meaning distorted. When he warned that if the Treaty were accepted, Volunteers trying to insure Irish freedom would have to wade through Irish blood, the press called his speech a cold incitement to civil war.

It was, of course, the exact opposite. De Valera was looking squarely at the situation in Ireland and reporting what he saw. The Irish Republican Army flatly refused to accept the Treaty. Most of its officers were determined to carry on their struggle to free Ireland from British domination. If the coming election went in favor of the Treaty, and the I.R.A. kept on its avowed course, then it must fight the pro-Treaty forces which Mulcahy, new Minister for Defense, was beginning to recruit.

Yet the Griffith supporter, P. S. O'Hegarty, wrote of that speech: "De Valera's gunmen had now received his blessing and they were free from any doubt as to how far he was prepared to go."

Nevertheless the Irish leaders that late winter and spring of 1922 were men of good will. Had they been left alone they might well have worked out their differences and reached the peaceful solution they all desired. But they were not left alone.

In February, the Sinn Fein convention brought to the country what seemed a hope for domestic peace. De Valera and Griffith spoke from the same platform. It was agreed that there would be no election for three months. And before the election, those who had signed the Treaty would draft a Constitution and present it to the people. Michael Collins promised that it would be a "Republican Constitution," and the convention adjourned in a renewed spirit of amity.

Apparently this was not what the British wanted, for immediately Winston Churchill, then Secretary of State for the Colonies, summoned Griffith to London. After their conference Churchill reported to the House of Commons that Griffith's opposition to the Irish Republicans was as strong as ever. That infuriated men of the Irish Republican Army. They said that Arthur Griffith was taking orders from the enemy, and proceeded to hold an Army Convention that had been prohibited by the Griffith Cabinet. During the convention they declared themselves henceforth under the sole control of an Army Executive Committee which they would elect themselves.

In April, the I.R.A. decided to establish a headquarters in the capital, and the next thing Dubliners knew, Rory O'Connor and his detachment had quietly taken possession of The Four Courts, the great building that housed Ireland's legal system, and were beginning to fortify it.

Perhaps an even unhappier man than Eamon de Valera during these troubled times was Michael Collins. Greatly as he admired Arthur Griffith, convinced as he was that the Treaty was Ireland's only hope at the moment, it must have gone against Collins' grain to be called to London as he frequently was and told what to do by leaders of the British Government.

Every officer of the I.R.A., arrayed now against Griffith's Provisional Government, had fought the British under Collins' direction. Harry Boland, probably Collins' closest friend, had gone body and soul over to de Valera.

Michael Collins had a soft heart for his friends. He had an especially tender feeling for children—all children. When five of the Catholic MacMahon family were slaughtered in Belfast, Collins got a photograph of the shambles and the next time he went to London threw it on the desk in front of Winston Churchill. It was said that Churchill burst into tears when he saw it. But the British Government still made no move to restrain the Ulster Specials. On the contrary, British Field Marshal Sir Henry Wilson, military advisor to the Belfast Government, encouraged its head, Sir James Craig, to strengthen his armed forces, and it seemed that every time Wilson made a speech, there was a fresh outburst of cruelty against the Catholics.

Perhaps Winston Churchill made some attempt to stop this persecution; at least, it was in his Colonial Offices in London that Michael Collins met with Sir James Craig to thrash out an agreement between their two governments. But although the document, signed by both men and countersigned by Churchill, began: "Peace is today declared," it was a peace of short duration, for the Belfast government either would not or could not control the men they had armed and encouraged to drive Catholics out of the Six Counties.

On the last day of May, two Ulster Specials were shot, possibly by some of the Irish Republican Army. In a vengeful fury, more of the Specials, in armored cars with machine guns chattering, roared up and down the streets of Belfast's Catholic section, breaking into houses and setting them afire, murdering their inhabitants, men and women alike. A few days later a Belfast mob fired through the windows of a Catholic hospital while patients cowered under their beds and frantic nurses and doctors ran to protect children wounded earlier in anti-Catholic pogroms.

These two vicious forays brought together the I.R.A. and the forces of Collins and Mulcahy. Army leaders of both factions decided that, even though Belfast and the border of the Six Counties were garrisoned by sixty thousand British troops, they must be attacked.

It was probably just what Sir James Craig and his military advisor, Wilson, were hoping the southern Irish would do. Both men wanted all Ireland under British rule. By their persecution of Belfast Catholics they were trying to goad the Republicans, who were mostly Catholics, into action against the British, an action they were confident must end in the reconquest of the whole country.

While the I.R.A. was compromising its differences, the political factions in Dublin had also made peace, short-lived though it proved to be. At the request of the Dail, Eamon de Valera was trying with Michael Collins to work out some kind of agreement that would heal the divisions among the deputies. As always, Dev had a plan, and Collins finally went along with it.

"The Collins–de Valera Pact" stated that the election, set for June 16, would not be for or against the Treaty, but for a Coalition Government with sixty-six pro-Treaty candidates, fifty-eight Republicans.

This pact was greeted throughout the country with acclaim. Even Arthur Griffith accepted it, albeit grudgingly. The British Cabinet were furious and denounced it as a violation of the Treaty, saying flatly that they would have nothing to do with any government that had de Valera in it.

Some time before, the Irish Constitution had been drawn up by Griffith and now had to be taken to London for approval. Instead of approving, the British changed it throughout, to bring it into harmony with their interpretation of the Treaty. Then Collins was summoned to England and when he came home again on election eve, he repudiated his pact with de Valera.

During the whole campaign the country was flooded with handbills threatening renewal of the Black and Tan savagery, return of the Auxiliaries, prison, executions, and "horrors which words cannot describe" unless the Treaty was ratified and only the pro-Treaty party elected.

In spite of solemn promises that it would be published well beforehand, the Irish people did not see their Constitution until the morning of election day. Most of them did not see it until after they had voted.

"So craven was this document," said Robert Briscoe, who

was to become Dublin's first Jewish Lord Mayor, "that Griffith and Collins dared not give Irishmen a chance to study it."

But the Irish were tired of trouble. They needed no posters to recall the black nights of the preceding years, the senseless murders, the harsh imprisonments. There was a desperate need for time to rebuild their ruined creameries, their burned-out shops and houses. For almost a year they had enjoyed the freedom of no curfews, no prowling spies, freedom to get together and gossip through a long summer evening. And Mick Collins was right, they said—the Treaty had got the British Army out of their towns and villages. For the first time in seven and a half centuries—since those first English invaders in 1171—a loyal Irishman could cheer when the British troops went by, for they were leaving! Soon they would be gone from all Ireland, or at least all free Ireland. . . .

Pro-Treaty men won fifty-eight seats. Eamon de Valera was elected, along with thirty-five other Republicans. Labour, the Farmers, Independents, and others made up the rest. Three quarters of the total were pledged to form the Coalition Government promised in the Collins–de Valera Pact, but it was not to materialize. The new Constitution which the people of Ireland sat down to read on election night provided that an oath of allegiance to the British King must be solemnly sworn by every member of the Irish Government before he could enter the Dail. What Republican could take such an oath? Griffith and Collins did not bother even to notify de Valera or anyone else in his party when the new Provisional Government would meet.

Suddenly the political situation was worse than ever, though the two I.R.A. factions continued to plan and plot together against the Belfast forces. But a third organization, the secret Irish Republican Brotherhood, gave orders concerning a plan made some time earlier, and a couple of

Michael Collins' men in London were designated to carry it out. Six days after the Irish election, they shot to death the man the I.R.B. considered to be the main instigator of the Belfast pogrom, British Field Marshal Sir Henry Wilson.

The two assassins were captured, but under questioning would only say that they had done the deed for Ireland. Arthur Griffith condemned their act as "anarchic." A statement from The Four Courts said flatly, "The shooting of Sir Henry Wilson was not done at the instance of the Irish Republican Army."

Calling the killing of a human being an awful act, Eamon de Valera said, "I do not know who they were who shot Sir Henry Wilson, or why they shot him. I know that life has been made a hell for the Nationalist [predominantly Catholic and anti-Treaty] minority in Belfast and its neighborhood for the past couple of years. . . . I do not approve, but I must not pretend to misunderstand."

But the British laid the whole blame on the Irish Republicans and, since the evacuation of British troops from Ireland had, by design, left sizable military forces in Dublin and at The Curragh, the Cabinet summoned English General Macready from Dublin and ordered him to mount an immediate attack on the Irish Republican Army headquarters in The Four Courts.

Macready was more intelligent than most of his countrymen. He knew that if he fired on Rory O'Connor's I.R.A. detachment, such action would unite both the factions of the Army against the British. He argued his case well. Lloyd George and Winston Churchill decided that Griffith's Provisional Government, just elected, must themselves order the attack.

Lloyd George wrote Michael Collins that unless he took strong and prompt action against the I.R.A. stronghold, the British would consider that the Treaty had been violated and take appropriate action. He offered whatever military assistance the Provisional Government might require.

Collins was away when this message was received in Dublin. On his return, he tried to temporize, asking for evidence that the Republicans were responsible for Wilson's murder. As Collins knew it must be, his request for evidence was refused, and the net of British coercion began to be drawn yet more tightly about the Irishmen who had signed the Treaty and were now at the head of the Irish Government.

Frustration—not knowing where to turn—often triggers an explosion out of all proportion to the situation. Michael Collins knew how unfair it was to blame the I.R.A. for the Wilson assassination, but he could not tell the British who had really been responsible. Besides, Rory O'Connor was getting too big for his britches. If the Irish were ever to achieve a stable government, he and other rebellious leaders of the I.R.A. had to be brought under control.

Arthur Griffith, whose compromise had avoided renewal of the war he dreaded with Britain, found rising in its place the more awful sight of Irishmen at one another's throats. He eased his anger cursing de Valera and at last said if his government was going to have to fight the Republicans, it might as well be now.

The correspondence with the British was kept secret and the Griffith government never admitted that it had received a demand from London to move against the Irish Republican Army. Instead, using the excuse that I.R.A. men had kidnaped an officer of the government army, Collins borrowed two eighteen-pounder field guns from the British and trained them on The Four Courts. At 3:40 A.M., Wednesday, June 28, 1922, Rory O'Connor's forces within the great building received a notice calling on them to surrender *within twenty minutes*. At seven minutes past four, the bombardment from the British guns began. And their first flashing roar sent Ireland tumbling over the precipice into civil war.

Later that morning Eamon de Valera's Model-T Ford bounced along the road from Greystones to Dublin. He knew nothing of the British ultimatum to Collins. He did not know who had ordered the assassination of Sir Henry Wilson. The I.R.A. leaders no longer took him into their confidence, and it had been a long time since the men of Griffith's Provisional Government had had anything to do with him. A man with a genius for compromise was in little demand that summer of 1922 in Ireland. He could not have been blamed if he had bundled up his family and gone off to America. But he still hoped that somehow he could help preserve the peace, quiet the Army hotheads. . . .

Before he had traveled a third of his way an old farmer hailed him with the awful news that the troops were shelling The Four Courts. "I wouldn't go on if I were you, sir," said the farmer. But de Valera's horror drove him forward. All the sacrifices, the striving, had been useless. The worst evil that could befall a country had come upon his Ireland. And he knew whom to blame.

As soon as he reached Dublin, he wrote:

At the last meeting of Dail Eireann, in a manifesto to the Irish people, an Agreement was ratified which, if faithfully observed, would have given us an opportunity of working for internal peace and of taking steps which would make this nation strong against the only enemy it has to fear—the enemy from outside. At the bidding of the English, Irishmen are today shooting down on the streets of our capital Irishmen—old comrades in arms, companions in the recent struggle for Ireland's independence and its embodiment—the Republic.

English propaganda will strive to lay the blame for this war on Irishmen, but the world outside must not be deceived. England's threat of war, and that alone, is responsible for the present situation. In face of England's threat some of our countrymen yielded. The men who are now being attacked by the forces of the Provisional Government are those who refuse to obey the order to yield—preferring to die.

The last line in that de Valera manifesto is the key to his next action: he reported for duty to his old Third Battalion. He had no hope that they would win. He expected to be killed. As a man of honor he could take no other course.

Continuing on its biased, bitter way, the press refused to publish de Valera's manifesto. Erskine Childers printed copies of it and distributed them, but their effect was lost in the torrent of invective poured out on de Valera by the press for daring to resist what he knew to be British-inspired oppression.

The army faction which had split with the I.R.A. now became known as the army of the Irish Free State, the area under control of Griffith's Provisional Government. This army was receiving quantities of British arms and ammunition, British artillery and ships with which to fight the I.R.A. It was also accepting into its ranks Irishmen whose only military training had been in the British Army, others who had served in the British police force—anyone, in fact, who cared to apply, no matter how great his former hostility to the cause of Irish freedom.

The siege of The Four Courts, completely one-sided, lasted only three days. With some of his men, Rory O'Connor was captured and imprisoned. But contrary to Collins' hopes, instead of ending the fighting, this only spread it through the city and out into the countryside.

In Republican headquarters, now moved to O'Connell Street, Eamon de Valera persuaded Cathal Brugha and some of the others to try at least once more for the truce with the Free State Army. He sent messages to both Collins and

Griffith asking an end to the fighting, promising that the Republican forces would leave their positions. He asked that Dail Eireann be assembled, and the differences among them be settled there. None of his requests were heeded. Bombardment of O'Connell Street was like that of the 1916 Rising. After five days of it, de Valera and some of the others escaped from their headquarters and left the area. With a small detachment, Cathal Brugha still held his post in the Hamman Hotel. The following day, it was set afire and his commanding officer ordered Brugha to surrender.

That night, as the roof of the hotel began to blaze, Brugha sent his men out to give themselves up. He stayed inside. He had decided long ago that death was preferable to surrender. At last, as the fire ate inexorably toward him, he flung open the door and rushed out, heading for the sandbagged post of the Free State troops, gun in hand, firing as he ran. "Stop!" cried his men, and one of the Free State officers, "Cathal—for God's sake, stop!" But Cathal Brugha, a smile on his face, went straight into the stream of bullets spitting from a machine gun. To stop men such as he it is necessary to kill them.

Michael Collins mourned Brugha's death, recognizing him ". . . among the very few who have given their all that this country—now torn by civil war—should have its freedom."

But the men in London felt no regret that their policy in regard to Ireland had driven her to civil war, was costing her the lives of brave and loyal men. Lord Birkenhead called the shelling of Dublin's most historic buildings a necessary operation and rejoiced that the task, "painful, costly, bloody as it must ultimately prove . . ." was being undertaken by Irishmen themselves, whose duty it was to undertake it.

Within a month, the gay, warm-hearted Harry Boland was arrested and, although unarmed, was shot in the stomach by an inexperienced young Free State soldier. His sister found him in a hospital, asked who had done it. He only shook his head and, dying, said, "Bury me beside Cathal Brugha."

The news of Harry Boland's death was slow in reaching Eamon de Valera, and he had not recovered from the shock of losing that good loyal friend when he learned of Arthur Griffith's death from a heart attack.

"It was a broken heart that killed him," said Michael Collins. And Dev forgot the trouble of the last few months between Griffith and himself, remembered the stanch and stubborn fighter for Ireland Arthur Griffith had been until the very last. And perhaps Dev wondered if, as with President Woodrow Wilson, Griffith's giving way under British pressure could be blamed in part at least on physical weakness that even he did not suspect.

By this time most Republicans were "on the run." The south and west of Ireland still championed their cause, but aided by floods of British war matériel and an unlimited supply of money, the Free State Army was gradually encircling the I.R.A. Eamon de Valera saw how hopeless it was to continue the fighting, but the Republican leaders would not listen to him. Helpless, hunted from place to place, he watched the growing horror, he said, as through "a wall of glass."

In his home county of Cork, Michael Collins, now Commander of the Free State Army, told a friend he too wanted to end the war.

"I'm going to see the Long Fellow and fix it up," said Collins.

"What about the British?" asked the friend.

"To hell with the British!" said Collins.

But two days later, driving along a lonely road, his convoy ran into a roadside ambush. Michael Collins was shot in the head and died instantly.

They brought his body back to Dublin and there he lay in state, mourned by thousands. And the Republicans should have regretted his death even more than Free Staters, for with Collins gone there was no one left on the Free State side with any thought of compromise, neither William Cosgrave (who became the head of the government), nor Richard Mulcahy, the Minister of Defense, nor the able Kevin O'Higgins, who was continuing his rise to power as Secretary for Home Affairs.

With Dail Eireann once more in session, the Irish people hoped that they would learn the reasons for some of the things that were going on. A Labor Deputy asked first what had led to the firing on Rory O'Connor's forces in The Four Courts. Richard Mulcahy said the action had been taken because Republican forces were about to strike at British military posts still remaining in the Free State.

From the prison where he had been held since June, O'Connor gave Mulcahy the lie, calling the hypocrisy of the Free State leaders astounding. But who was to pay attention to anything O'Connor said? Along with all Republicans he was labeled rebel and traitor by the Irish press.

Like all civil wars, the war in Ireland inevitably became one of personalities. Erskine Childers had only a small hand press on which to print the Republican side of the bitter dispute, but at least one of the Free State leaders proved as sensitive to Childers' criticism as Arthur Griffiths' had been. Calling Childers "an Englishman," and "leader of those opposed to this government," Kevin O'Higgins accused him of striking deadly blows at the economic life of the nation.

In November, on his way to Dublin where he had been summoned by Eamon de Valera, Childers was captured at the home of his cousin, Robert Barton. The day after his arrest, Winston Churchill referred to him as a "mischief-making, murderous renegade," and it was clear that no matter how great his contribution to Irish freedom, this gentle man would not be spared. Three weeks later, convicted of possession of an automatic pistol (which Michael Collins had given him), Erskine Childers was shot at dawn in Beggars Bush Barracks.

By the first week in December the whole Free State was under martial law. On December 7, when a government deputy who had voted for martial law was killed on a Dublin street, General Mulcahy asked permission from the Free State Cabinet to shoot four Republican prisoners as reprisal for his death. And although members of the Cabinet well knew that such reprisal was not only barbaric but also quite illegal, Mulcahy got his permission. Next morning four young men who had spent their whole lives working and fighting for Irish independence were wakened, told to prepare themselves for death and within a few hours were shot in the yard at Mountjoy Jail. Rory O'Connor was one of them.

The question will be asked until the end of Irish history: Why those four? Was someone fearful what they might tell, one day? The men of the I.R.A. were so enraged by the executions that they hurled themselves into a reckless program of ambush, house-burning and destruction of property. But at the beginning of the New Year more Republican prisoners were executed. By the end of January, fifty-five had been shot by Free State firing squads.

As in the fight between North and South in the United States sixty years before, civil war was bringing out the worst in the Irish. They filled the concentration camps, overcrowded the jails. Abuse of prisoners, torture, murder after surrender were common. But no matter how unprincipled the government, there was no winning a war against it without the support of the people. And the people were too exhausted and terrified to resist longer.

Eamon de Valera finally persuaded the I.R.A. to dump their arms, telling them that they could no longer successfully defend the Republic.

"Seven years of intense effort have exhausted our people,"

he wrote. "If they have turned aside and have not given you the active support which alone could bring you victory in this last year it is because they saw overwhelming forces against them, and they are weary and need a rest. . . . The sufferings which you must now face unarmed, you will bear in a manner worthy of men who were ready to give their lives for their cause. . . . May God guard every one of you. . . ."

Free State President William Cosgrave accepted May 12, 1923, as the date when disturbances should come to an end, but arrests in the name of the government continued long after that. By July 1 there were 11,316 military prisoners; of that number 250 were women. With the war over, their detention was illegal, but Cosgrave hurried another Public Safety Act through the Dail, permitting the government to keep on making arrests and holding anyone it saw fit for as long a time as it cared to do so.

Cosgrave called a free, general election for August 27. Eamon de Valera, nominated for his old constituency in East Clare, was threatened with imprisonment if he appeared.

"If the people of Clare elect me as their candidate," he said, "I will be with them, and nothing but a bullet will stop me."

ON AUGUST 15 DE VALERA WILL SPEAK IN ENNIS! said the posters.

Free State Army troops and droves of secret service men thronged the town to see that he did not. The people had little hope that their Dev would be able to make his way into the town, but they came out of the hills by car, by donkey cart, and on foot to crowd its narrow streets.

There were thundering cheers when his tall, thin figure appeared on the platform in the marketplace. Touched and grateful to the point of tears, he began speaking. But two files of soldiers with fixed bayonets forced their way through the crowd, followed by an armored car on which a machine gun was mounted. The soldiers fired above the heads of the townspeople. Blank shot, they said later, although two men and a woman were wounded by it.

"Stop! Stop!" cried de Valera, but he could not make himself heard and someone—perhaps trying to protect him—threw him down on the platform. He struggled to his feet. As his head and shoulders emerged above the group on the platform, a wave of cheering louder than before swept the crowded streets.

But he saw that the soldiers were about to fire again. Putting aside the friendly hands that tried to stop him, Eamon de Valera descended from the platform and submitted to arrest.

"The heights by great men gained and kept
Were not attained by sudden flight,
But they, while their companions slept,
Were toiling upward in the night."
  Henry Wadsworth Longfellow

12

LONG ROAD BACK

THERE IS A cardinal rule of politics which reads, *Never im-
prison your opponent; it gives him time to think.*

Either William Cosgrave never heard of the rule or he
chose to ignore it. He had Eamon de Valera shut up in Arbor
Hill Prison and the following week made a speech in County
Clare, ridiculing de Valera and making it clear that he believed they had seen the last of him, politically speaking.

"He is fairly safe . . ." taunted Cosgrave. "Bullet did not
stop him. Blank cartridge was enough . . ."

But the people of County Clare said, "What did Mr. Cosgrave mean when he promised a free election?" And they reminded one another, "We voted for Dev when he was in an
English prison." And they said, "Remember, in 1917, how
de Valera insisted on sharing the platform with this same
Professor Eoin MacNeill who is running against him now?"

And some of them, remembering the reprisal executions
of other Republican leaders without charge or trial, said un-
easily, "What did Mr. Cosgrave mean, that our Dev is 'fairly
safe'?"

On election day, Eamon de Valera got more than twice the votes given to his opponent. But this time there was no "putting him in to get him out." He was kept in solitary confinement, in a cell sixteen feet by eight, with only one small window, high in the wall.

"I think," he said many years later, "they were afraid I might contaminate someone."

News of his election eventually came to him. His guards, hostile at first, grew to admire their prisoner who did not complain and never asked for special favors. But as fall chilled into winter the lines deepened in Dev's face. He worried about Sinead and the children, wondered about Terry, the baby he had never seen, who would be a year old in December of this sad, tragic year of 1923. Except for young Vivion, brought in for a brief visit while Dev was in hiding, he had not seen any of his family since the dark June morning when the bombardment of The Four Courts marked the beginning of Ireland's futile civil war.

The Cosgrave government continued to lay the entire blame for the conflict on de Valera's shoulders, calling him "the man who cost the country a civil war and seventeen million pounds."

If the Long Fellow had been a despairing man, the imprisonment would have finished him. He had given heart and mind and body to Ireland. This was his reward, a cell as dank and forbidding as could be found in any English jail. Thousands of his fellow Republicans were behind bars, hundreds of them on hunger strike, until the government made it plain that, unlike their British captors of two years before, leaders of the Irish Free State would let the prisoners die rather than release them.

Sometime during the winter de Valera was taken from Arbor Hill. He was to be the last of the "long procession of patriots" whose ghosts haunt the cells of Kilmainham Jail. He must have wondered at the transfer, remembering that it was here the leaders of the Rising were taken to be executed.

Kilmainham was dark, and from its stone floors seeped a paralyzing chill. Dev's long arms could almost touch his cell walls from side to side. Two strides of his long legs from end to end would have sent him crashing into damp stone. He strained his eyes to read until all light was gone. In the endless nights he prayed for the souls of men and women who had preceded him to this grim place.

There had been no crash of combat to sustain the Irish patriot here, no friendly comrade to encourage him—only the threats of icy water in a tank where he must stand neck-deep, a black cell totally without light, a padded cell should he be driven mad, as many were, and at last, a wall to brace himself against as he faced a firing squad, or a slow march toward a looped rope dangling from the gallows.

But to Eamon de Valera, who knew his history, there was no spot in all Ireland where more gallant and unwavering commitments to the cause of Irish freedom had been made. And in the dark and cold and loneliness, he renewed his own.

He lost faith neither in Ireland nor in his destiny. He was a teacher and, discovering that the guard who brought his meals could neither read nor write, he volunteered to show him how. The first word his pupil learned to spell may still be seen scratched into the stone of the Kilmainham corridor: COLLIᴙS—the diagonal of the N first slanted backward, ᴙ, then scratched in properly when he learned how it should look.

More closely than ever before, Dev began to study his political opponents. Many of those who differed with him were sincere, that was certain. Some lacked good judgment. Most of them seemed blind to the way Ireland was sliding slowly but inevitably back under British rule.

That year spring was long in coming, but one morning, pacing round a stone circle in a small, high-walled yard, he heard the stirring sound of far-off trumpets—not those of brass, but wild geese—and looked up to see an arrow of them flying north. It is an Irish fancy to recall men who fled death and Irish famine into exile, to say their souls return as wild geese to circle over Ireland, to spiral down and float on waters of her lakes and rivers, home at last. This morning, seeing those free voyagers stream across the sky set a desire for escape swelling in Eamon de Valera's heart until he needed his narrow cell again to recover self-control.

Not until spring had passed and sunny days were ripening the harvest did the Cosgrave government decide their solitary prisoner was dead for once and all in Irish politics. On July 24 they released him, sent him home.

Heaven and hell could hold no greater contrast than that between the dreary limits of Kilmainham and the sun-bathed space and fresh sea wind that welcomed him at Greystones. There were the children to get acquainted with all over again, and Sinead with tears of happiness in her blue eyes, grown more beautiful than ever. The baby, Terry, was a handful—spoiled a little, but it was the nature of women to spoil their youngest. His father laughed to hear him talk, see him go crawling up the stairs, lively as a young pup. What a blessing to laugh again!

Dev walked the shore, breathing the salt air till it banished the last vestige of the acrid, hopeless prison smell that lingered in his nostrils. And soon, because so much time had been wasted, he gathered about him the remnants of Sinn Fein, with some comrades from the Irish Republican Army, and together they took a hard look at their country.

Because they would not take the Oath of Allegiance to the British King, neither Dev nor any other Republican was allowed to take the seats in Dail Eireann to which they had been elected. But they could watch what went on there.

The Cosgrave forces had been working without success to abolish Partition and bring Belfast and the Six Counties of the northeast into an all-Ireland Parliament, as Free State leaders thought had been planned for in the Treaty with the British. Those Six Counties had been hurriedly thrown into the Belfast area when Lloyd George set up his Better Government of Ireland Act in 1920. Even he had not expected the Six Counties to remain an entity, since two of them, Tyrone and Fermanagh, were almost entirely populated by Catholics and Irish Nationalists who wished to be reunited with their compatriots in the south.

Michael Collins had written "Under the Treaty, Ireland is about to become a fully constituted nation. . . . The whole of Ireland, *as one nation,* is to compose the Irish Free State. . . ."

Now, how was that to come about, with Britisher Sir James Craig in Belfast, declaring he'd give up not a single inch?

Collins had thought he knew: "If [the Six Counties of Ulster] stay out, the decision of the Boundary Commission arranged for in the Treaty would be certain to deprive Ulster of Fermanagh and Tyrone. Shorn of these counties she would shrink to insignificance. . . ."

In September, following his release from prison, Eamon de Valera made a speech in Cork during which he read a letter written to him by Arthur Griffith during the Treaty negotiations. The British Prime Minister had promised, Griffith said, that if the men of Belfast refused to cooperate with the Boundary Commission, he, Lloyd George, would "fight, summon Parliament, appeal to it against Ulster, dissolve, or pass an Act establishing an All-Ireland Parliament."

But Griffith and Collins were dead. Lloyd George no longer was in office. It was the autumn of 1924, and as the British brought up their heavy political guns, all of them thundered in favor of Sir James Craig's control of the northeast of Ireland.

Dev had always been suspicious of that Boundary Commission clause in the Treaty, in which Collins had put so much trust. But now anyone who even suggested that it might be the Free State that would be trimmed by the Boundary Commission, not the Six Counties, was due for a stiff, official reproof from Kevin O'Higgins.

"Unlike you," he said to one such doubter in his own party, "I still hope for a straight deal. . . ."

But on November 7 a story broke in the bitterly anti-Irish *Morning Post,* saying the Boundary Commission had decided that no territory was to be transferred to the Free State except slim strips of land in Fermanagh and Armagh (counties bordering on the south). And worse—Craig's Belfast Government was to take over a tract of the richest land in County Donegal which, up to now, had been in the Free State.

It was, thought de Valera, the 1691 Treaty of Limerick all over again, signed in good faith at the time, perhaps, but broken as soon as it was to England's advantage to do so.

Cosgrave and O'Higgins went rushing off to London. If the newspaper account had been accurate, if they could not salvage something from this Boundary mess, the Free State party was finished politically in Ireland.

Eamon de Valera warned the Irish people what would happen.

"They will leave the Boundary as it is," he said. "In other words, the people of South Down, South Armagh, Derry City, as well as of Tyrone and Fermanagh, are to be sacrificed, although it was on the plea of saving them that the Treaty was carried."

On the third of December a telegram came from Cosgrave and O'Higgins, heralding a new agreement which they confidently recommended to the Irish people. "Today," they said, "we have sown the seeds of peace."

They had done exactly what Dev had said they would do, signed over the whole Six Counties of the northeast to the

Belfast Government. They claimed, however, to have persuaded the British to cancel the financial liability of the Irish Free State. Cosgrave boasted later that the agreement was "a damn good bargain . . ."

De Valera wondered. If it were such a good bargain for the Irish, why had the British Parliament approved the agreement with such alacrity? True, most of their leaders rejoiced to see Sir James Craig firmly established in the north, but there was more than a slight smell of fish about the whole transaction. Besides, even if it were to the Free State's financial advantage, what about the thousands of loyal Irish it had violently separated from the Free State against their will?

"I had hoped," wrote de Valera, "that no Irishman, North or South, would be found prepared to put his hand to an instrument dismembering his country."

The Irish Labor party published a furious manifesto calling the agreement "an unmitigated betrayal," but their votes were too few to block it and the Republican deputies had no votes at all since they were still kept from their rightful places in the Dail by that abhorred oath to the British King. The agreement was approved, 71 votes to 20.

The fishy smell grew stronger. In spite of Cosgrave's protestation that everything was settled between England and the Free State, within three months representatives of the two countries signed a secret agreement by which the Irish must pay the British the full amount of the Land Purchase Annuities—money advanced, back in de Valera's boyhood, to enable Irish farmers to purchase land from British landlords.

Suddenly the man the Free State Cabinet believed they had discredited in everyone's eyes came very much alive. In spite of the fact that "De Valera was a leader without an army, without a voice in Parliament, without funds," as a disillusioned Irish historian wrote, and that his Dublin office was a cramped and gloomy space, as his friend Robert Briscoe described it, there was no feeling of despair in those dingy rooms. For Eamon de Valera was planning for the future.

He had decided to enter the Dail, if some way could be found to do so without taking an oath to the King. One would have thought that was a goal which could be supported by any friend of his—and Ireland's—but it set off a ruckus in the ranks of Sinn Fein that broke the party wide open. At the party convention, when the vote was taken on his proposed course, de Valera and his moderates were defeated 223 to 218.

It was Dev's habit to let everyone have his say during debate on any question. Once a decision was made, however, he never felt bound to go along with the majority unless he felt also that they had made the right decision. In this case, he made no attempt to change the minds of the majority in Sinn Fein. He simply resigned from the organization and formed a new political party, calling it the Army of Destiny —in Gaelic, *Fianna Fail.*

He moved out of the Sinn Fein offices. He could afford no others, but somehow his followers got enough money together to rent two rooms over a jewelry shop on O'Connell Street. Hope was burgeoning in men who had thought never to hope again. At the first Fianna Fail convention, five hundred jammed the La Scala Theater, welcoming de Valera as if he were an angel sent from heaven to their aid.

He had no easy solutions for their problems. His primary aim, to remove the Oath of Allegiance to the British Crown, promised to be difficult indeed for Cosgrave and O'Higgins swore that if the Oath were tampered with, there would be an inevitable return to armed conflict with the British.

But Dev had searched for loopholes in the documents by which the Free State Cabinet ruled. He thought he had found one that would enable the Irish to rid themselves not only of the oath, but the British Governor-General. It was simply, he said, to amend the Constitution!

As for the Land Annuities, Fianna Fail should put a stop to those payments. They were, said Dev, illegal. England had officially renounced them once. She could give them up again, forever. Then, if any *just* debts were owed the British, Ireland should pay them immediately.

Then, he said, Ireland must become self-sufficient, and unfolded a scheme that reminded his listeners of the early days of Sinn Fein, when the young men of the west marched with pipes and drum to divide vast tracts of grassland so that the farmers might grow grain.

He had more plans. His mind teemed with them. Paramount, of course, was his hope of ending Partition. But before Fianna Fail could succeed in any of these noble undertakings, they had to have funds.

Dev got them in New York, where a judge had ordered Irish bond money returned to the subscribers. Many generously gave the cash directly to de Valera, and back he came to Ireland, not only to launch Fianna Fail with a grand splash, but to found a desperately needed newspaper. And then he plunged into a campaign for the election to be held in June 1927.

Although posters threatened return of the British if Fianna Fail got into office, the Irish people had heard the threat so often it no longer registered. Fianna Fail won forty-four seats to Cosgrave's forty-six. But as Dev led his delegates to the Dail, they were turned away, for they still refused to swear allegiance to the British King. De Valera had been right about the ease of amending the Constitution to get rid of that oath, but why should the Free Staters do him any favors, when he seemed apt to turn them out of power if they did?

Then came a tragedy which no one could foresee and all regretted. As in every country after a civil war, Ireland was plagued with men refusing to obey a government which they despised, who took the law in their own hands and acted as judge, jury, and executioner if someone displeased them. In Dublin, on his way to Mass one sunny morning, Kevin O'Higgins was assassinated. His murderers escaped and for a while it looked as if every member of Fianna Fail would be arrested for questioning.

Dev came home from Clare to find an armed guard placed before his house by the government. At once he issued a statement denying that any member of Fianna Fail had anything to do with O'Higgins' murder. Dev sympathized with those whose ideal was still an Irish Republic, and because they were true to that ideal, were refused a voice in government. But that was no excuse for lawless violence. It was time for an end to that in Ireland.

Now, as if to make sure de Valera and his party would remain forever out of power, President Cosgrave introduced a law which would force every candidate for the Dail to declare *in advance* that if elected, he would take the oath to the British King. Realizing that, unless he blocked the new law, none of his followers could even run for office, Eamon de Valera courageously declared that Fianna Fail members would enter the Dail, at once. He said that the oath to the British Crown had become an empty formula, but all Fianna Fail deputies must be careful to push the Bible aside, and announce that in signing they accepted no obligation and took no oath.

Amid jeers from the frustrated Cosgrave party, Eamon de Valera led his deputies down the steep red-carpeted stairs to the benches where seats awaited them. At once the Labor party proposed a vote of "No Confidence" in the government. The vote was a tie, broken in Cosgrave's favor by the Speaker of the House, but Cosgrave dissolved the Dail and called another general election.

This time Fianna Fail gained thirteen seats, giving them a total of fifty-seven. Cosgrave's party got sixty-one. Both had gained at the expense of smaller parties. De Valera was content to lead the Opposition for a while. He realized that his men needed experience and assigned each a special project, to study every department of government and try to discover how it could be better administered.

Cosgrave's party survived the election of 1927, but four years later his majority was reduced to three and again he dissolved the Dail and called an election. This one was fought on de Valera's chosen grounds: abolishing the Oath of Allegiance, the retention of the Land Annuities, the release of Republican prisoners held under a coercive Public Safety Act passed the year before.

For the first time, Fianna Fail had the help of a friendly newspaper, Dev's *Irish Press*. And de Valera himself headed into the 1932 campaign with all the verve of a young man running for his first public office.

On election eve, as the last bonfire guttered low, de Valera was fresher than his exhausted followers. One of them recalled a quotation that Mrs. Dev was fond of:

"There is a time in the affairs of men which, taken at the flood, leads on to fortune. . . ."

Somehow that night they all felt that de Valera's tide, at last, was at the flood.

"Ireland her own and all therein, from the sod to the sky;
the soil of Ireland for people of Ireland to have and to
hold from God alone who gave it; to have and to hold for
them and their heirs forever, without suit or service, rent or
render, faith or fealty, to any power under heaven. . . ."
James Fintan Lalor—Nineteenth Century

13

ARMY OF

DESTINY

PRESS RELEASE—LONDON—MARCH 12, 1932.

The new Irish President is only a temporary interruption, a
nerveless, romantic, grandiloquent half-Irish Kerensky, who will
soon be shattered by the harsh realities of the world.

After years of seeing Eamon de Valera belittled by his own
countrymen, this was not a surprising reaction from a British
newspaper when news came that Fianna Fail had taken over
the Irish government and Eamon de Valera was the new
president of the Executive Council.

His party had not won a clear majority, but Labor voted
with Fianna Fail to make Dev president. And he launched
his program with as much assurance as if he had been elected
by 100 per cent of the voters.

It suited de Valera's fancy to announce the first step of that
program in a St. Patrick's Day radio speech to the land of

his birth, the United States. He was, he said, about to abolish the hated Oath of Allegiance to the British Crown.

Fortunately, the Statute of Westminster (which the Cosgrave government had helped to pass) furnished Dev with the means of getting rid of the Oath. That amused him, for during the last twelve years, he considered that Cosgrave had used the Oath for his own political advantage.

Dev paid no heed to the rumbles from England that greeted his announcement. On April 5 he went on to say exactly what he thought of the Treaty of 1921 and its consequences. The Irish had agreed to it, he said, only under a threat of immediate and terrible war. The British had no right to partition Ireland against her will, to collect Land Annuities to which they were not entitled, or to be in possession of Irish ports.

This speech brought an old adversary out of retirement. On June 17, Lloyd George said in the British House of Commons that he was startled by the fact that two British Cabinet members had actually gone to Dublin to confer with de Valera on these matters.

"I have had some experience with Mr. de Valera as a negotiator," said the former Prime Minister, "and frankly, I have never seen anything like him. Mr. de Valera is perfectly unique, and the poor distracted world has a good right to be profoundly thankful that he is unique."

Laughter swept the chamber, but his audience sobered as Lloyd George made a statement concerning the substance of Mr. de Valera's demand in 1921:

"His demand was not that Ireland should be a part of the British Commonwealth of Nations with such rights as each Dominion has . . . but that Ireland should be a Sovereign State. . . . He has not changed one iota of that position, and let us not treat that as if it were merely a trumpery question of the Oath. . . .

"He will never change," cried Lloyd George, shaking back

his mane of white hair, "right to the end. He has always turned back to the past like a pillar of salt and you cannot make him do otherwise!"

There was more, a good deal more, but the part of the speech which impressed the Irish people was Lloyd George's acknowledgment that their Dev had never strayed from his avowed course of action.

Dail Eireann passed a bill to abolish the Oath, but the measure was held up in the Irish Senate by amendments which the Dail refused to accept. According to the Constitution, however, unless there were another election, the bill would become law in eighteen months.

President de Valera was not so peremptory when it came to the Land Annuities. He discussed them in Dublin with J. H. Thomas, Britain's Dominions Secretary, and when they could not agree, suggested that the question be submitted to arbitration. That was fine with Thomas, but of course the arbitrators must be chosen from within the British Empire.

"Ah, no," said de Valera. This dispute was between two nations. If it went to arbitration, it must be before an international tribunal.

Horrified at the suggestion, Thomas went back to London shaking his head, and reported that the Irish Government was acting as if agreements between it and the British did not exist. De Valera wanted the Free State and Northern Ireland reunited, said Thomas. And he wanted recognition of Ireland as a Republic. Protesting that the Irish had no mandate for such a course, Thomas complained that nevertheless they were going to keep the Land Annuities.

And sure enough, on the first day of July the Land Annuities payment was not, as it had been since 1923, sent to England, but reserved in a special fund in Dublin.

Promptly the British Parliament levied customs duties on imports from Ireland. So began an economic war between the two countries, for Ireland retaliated in kind.

The year 1932 would always be remembered as the nadir of
the Great Depression, which had been spreading around the
world since the financial crash in America in 1929. Irish
exports to England had been gradually declining during
those years, so the customs duties were not so much of a
shock to the Irish as they would otherwise have been. However, they gave de Valera's opponents a good excuse to storm
at him. And he decided to go for support directly to Irish
farmers, the people who were being hurt the worst by the
British tariffs.

He felt at home with country people. And they seemed to
gain fresh hope the moment they saw Dev's tall figure loom-
ing above the others on any platform. He was as unchanging
as the seasons, and the farmers welcomed it when he urged
them as of old to make Ireland a self-sufficient nation, to
plow up their pastures and grow grain. . . .

This country, he said, had been a grazing ranch for feeding
others, a dumping ground for the manufactured goods of
others, a country whose people were brought up, like its livestock, for export. It would be far better for farmers and for
the country if they turned from growing cattle to growing
wheat. It would not be easy, but if they stood by the government, the government would stand by them. . . .

De Valera went back to Dublin to await results. He had
faith in the Irish people. He believed they would tighten
their belts and stand firm in this crisis, as he had so often
seen them do before. But in any case, he had no time to worry
about it. He had an important engagement in Switzerland.

Because of his almost universally bad press, de Valera was
still considered by the British people and their leaders a
sort of ludicrous Pat-and-Mike stage Irishman, bothersome at
times but of no more importance than a barfly. Few British
paid any attention to the announcement that the head of the
Irish delegation would preside in September 1932 over the
Thirteenth Meeting of the Assembly of the League of Na-

tions. Ireland had been a member of the League since 1923, although her status there had never been clearly defined. Most of the League members would have scorned the notion that any idea out of Ireland could impress their august gathering.

"The Irish, eh?" whispered a delegate. "They've brought their weather with them." Wind moaned in the chimneys and rain flooded the windows in a heavy autumn storm as Eamon de Valera rose to address them.

It took but a few words to make every delegate straighten in shocked amazement. For Dev had torn up the speech prepared for him, and in simple, straightforward language told that world body just what he thought of it.

The League of Nations had no power, he said, except that granted it by world opinion. Now people were looking at the League, wondering in this time of testing whether it would be weak or strong. Many of them felt that it was devoting itself to minor matters, disregarding the vitally important problems of the time. There was one effective way to silence such criticism: say that the Covenant of the League was a solemn pact, that no state, great or small, might ignore its obligations.

He spoke of the twenty-five million unemployed in the world, crying out for the right to work and stay alive, of a hundred million people starving in the midst of a world of plenty. And, at last, he spoke of Ireland:

"I want you to believe that we in Ireland desire peace—at home and throughout the world," said de Valera earnestly. "In spite of opinions you may have formed from misleading reports, I want you to know that our history is the history of a people who have consistently sought merely to be allowed to live their own lives in their own way, at peace with their neighbors and with the world.

"If we are left free, our way will be a way of peace, thinking in terms not of self-interest nor of the acquisition of territory nor of petty power . . . but of human beings living as they have a right to live in the best our State can give them, while contributing to the world the best that is in us." He looked down at the British delegate for an instant, then went on in the same calm, dispassionate voice, "I feel that other States could face the task in a similar spirit and with equal hope. . . ."

And after a formal concluding sentence, President de Valera said in Gaelic, "May God assist us in the exalted task before us, and may He not permit that we should fail."

There had been dead silence when he rose to speak. There was silence so utter when he finished, the delegates heard only the rain lashing at the windows. They were stunned by his candor. Many were quite unable to reconcile this deliberate, reasoning, dignified figure with the apish caricature that had been presented in British and Irish newspapers for the last ten years and more.

If the delegates were silent, newspapermen were not. They raced for their typewriters and telephones and the following day praise for the Irish President was read throughout the world.

"I heard this man eleven years ago speaking in the Dail, which was then still an Assembly of rebel conspirators, a good third of whom could share the tragic honor that an English court-martial had accorded him."

So read a dispatch from a Swiss correspondent, who then proceeded to paint a glowing picture of his subject:

"De Valera has changed but slightly since then. His keen sea-hawk features have not become hardened by the terrible experience of civil war, but only calmer and more decided. And now, as then, he speaks in a voice that has no seducingly melodious tones, but is matter-of-fact and earnest, with a much greater restraint in expression than might be expected of the adventurous leader, the conspirator and agitator, who has waged war against the might of England, with such simplicity of feeling as has been shown by no other living man, not even Gandhi."

The Manchester *Guardian* correspondent sent a less extravagant but just as enthusiastic report, calling de Valera's speech the best ever made by a President of the League Assembly.

"It was inspired by a true international spirit," wrote the reporter, "and for the first time a President asked the members of the League to face the reality that the world has a less high opinion of them than they have of themselves. Perhaps it was for that reason that the speech was not applauded. . . ."

So the chorus of approval spread into England. And many British people wondered greatly about this Irish rebel, being praised as a statesman whose stature was recognized in all the world.

Fame or no fame, the same problems awaited Dev at home as had been there when he left. During the campaign Fianna Fail had deplored the exorbitant cost of the governor-generalship, whose salary and expenses were estimated at somewhere between twenty and thirty thousand pounds a year. De Valera had averred that the office should be abolished with the Oath of Allegiance. In October the Governor-General was dismissed. To the amusement of the Irish and consternation of the British, a veteran of the 1916 Rising was appointed in his place—Donal Buckley, who had his own ideas of the duties and prerogatives of the office. He refused to move into the stately home in Phoenix Park and contented himself with a fraction of the former salary.

As a man who had, from the first, supported the Irish Republic, it must have given Buckley a great deal of satisfaction to sign into law the bill which finally abolished the Oath of Allegiance. This did not happen until the spring following his appointment, for an election had intervened and made it necessary for the bill to be introduced again in the Dail.

The Irish Republican Army was still going on frequent rampages through the country. De Valera had felt that once rid of the Oath so despised by the I.R.A. its members would cease their lawless behavior. To his disappointment they continued their forays, and because he hesitated to invoke the Cosgrave government's harsh measures against the rebels, all their misdeeds were blamed on him.

"I do not believe any man since Cromwell has inflicted more harm on this country," stormed one of Dev's political opponents.

In the fall of 1933, following more I.R.A. outrages, a speaker trying to address a meeting in Tralee was hit on the head with a hammer. When twelve I.R.A. members were arrested, tried, and sentenced, even though it was only to terms of four to six months in jail, there was a great roar of protest. On December 17, therefore, de Valera went to Tralee and told the people that he had a long and painful list of things that had happened there within the last three months.

"The only names I can honestly give to such acts are outrages and crimes," he said. "Houses have been fired into and it is a miracle that nobody was killed. Property has been willfully destroyed. Organized groups have taken it upon themselves to decide without any legal or moral right whatever how much liberty their fellow citizens must enjoy. Are the people going to surrender their right to decide *at the ballot box* what policy is best in the country's interests and what government shall rule?"

But although the furor in Tralee subsided, the I.R.A.— or some who labeled themselves members—continued to harass the de Valera government as they had harassed Cosgrave's. As in many secret military organizations, the rank and file were not subject to control from their officers. There had been, from the beginning, idealists in the ranks of the Irish Republican Army, but there were also fanatics and a few thieves and murderers. Since they struck without warning, wore no uniforms, and could seldom be identified, few were ever captured, much less prosecuted. At last, Dev was forced to use a military tribunal to deal with them.

Opposition to de Valera came from another quarter with organization by an Irish general of a National Guard, called because of their uniforms the Blue Shirts. Seeing this as just one more split in the armed forces of the country, de Valera brought into the Dail a bill to restrict the wearing of uniforms and make the raising of private armies an offense against the law.

"The time has come to end this tomfoolery of Blue-Shirt-ing," declared an indignant Dev, and he ridiculed the notion that this was a force whose aim was to save Ireland from communism.

"This country is not a natural breeding ground for com-munism and everybody knows it," he said. "It is opposed to our religion; it is opposed to our individualistic tendencies; it is opposed to our whole scheme of life. If there is one country in the world which is unsuitable soil for communism, it is this. . . ."

He appealed to all parties not to allow a condition of af-fairs to arise similar to that which preceded their civil war.

"We are relatively young," he pleaded. "Every member on the opposite benches and on these benches could, if driven to it, be an active participant in a physical conflict today. I ask deputies on the opposite benches not to do this thing. . . ."

Pointing out that the Blue Shirts had preached the doc-trines of German and Italian fascism, he said some of them were anti-Semites who had declared that he, de Valera, was a Jew. While denying it, he also wanted everyone to be sure that he had never been one to attack the Jewish people, or to condone such action.

Back of Dev on the Fianna Fail benches was Robert Bris-coe. As a Jew, he could testify that this man he called chief would rather die himself than permit people of any religion to be persecuted.

But there was an allegation to be met, and Dev was meeting it. He traced his lineage and his Catholic heritage, his baptism and his childhood in a Catholic home. Then with emotion contorting his body he cried, "I have lived amongst the Irish people and loved them, and loved every blade of grass that grew in this land. I do not care who says or who tries to pretend that I am not Irish. I say I have been known to be Irish and that I have given everything in me to the Irish nation!"

The fire in him swayed the Dail. His Uniform Restriction Bill was passed and sent to the Senate. There it was endlessly debated. He made a stormy attack on the senators, but it had no effect. They rejected the bill 30 to 18.

The day after he lost that battle, Eamon de Valera introduced in the Dail a bill to abolish the Senate. In due course it was to become law and the recalcitrant members of the Upper House could no longer—in de Valera's view—obstruct the progress of the country. But abolition of the Senate was yet two years away, and those two years were momentous ones for Ireland. Of course, during that period the Senate did not by any means bar all progress by the government.

Gradually a number of the old diehard Sinn Feiners began to see de Valera's side of things. After all, he had obtained for Ireland almost all they had been fighting for—except the wiping out of that one big aching scar of Partition. The Blue Shirts kept stirring things up, though, and in 1935 a Catholic bishop in Cork said grimly, "I see a country becoming torn by political hatreds. I see class war and faction war."

In spite of opposition at home, Eamon de Valera's personal fortunes continued to climb. Late in 1935 he spoke again to the Assembly of the League of Nations, this time in regard to the war which Italy was carrying into Ethiopia. The bonds between Ireland and Italy had always been strong and close, but Dev pledged his country to stand by its obligations under the Covenant of the League, and supported sanctions against Italy for her aggression. For this he was attacked by William Cosgrave and his Free Staters, but Dev had done what he knew to be right and the criticism bothered him not a bit.

He was, he felt, the most fortunate of men. He often looked at his fine family and thanked God that all had been spared, that Sinead's courage had never faltered. She scoffed if anyone mentioned the trials she had endured, saying stanchly, "I have my husband and my children. Others lost everyone they loved."

They had reason to be proud of the children. Vivion was studying law, Eamon was in medical school. Maureen was as serious a student as either of them. She had won honors throughout school and was working toward a Master's Degree in science. The three youngest, Rory, Emer, and Terry, were just as bright and eager to outdo one another. As for Brian, that gay, good-looking young fellow loved horses and people almost alike. In 1936, one gusty, soft February morning his father waved him off for a ride in Phoenix Park with his cousin. It was quite beyond belief later that day when an aide put his hand on Eamon de Valera's arm and told him Brian was badly hurt. His horse had bolted from the path; an overhanging branch had caught him on the head. The boy lived only a few hours.

Perhaps the tragedy endeared Eamon de Valera even more to a nation that had known so much suffering. He spent even a greater amount of time than before in his work of government. And the following December he found an opportunity to take his people a little farther along the path to Irish independence.

After the death of the British King in January 1936, King Edward VIII had come to the throne. His reign lasted less than a year, for in December he announced his abdication. According to laws of the Commonwealth, the Parliaments of the Dominions must agree to the accession of the new King, George VI.

The Irish Parliament agreed—on their own terms—recognizing King George as head of the British Commonwealth but not as King of Ireland. Henceforth the Irish would consult him only on external matters. To read of this must have made old Lloyd George twist his white mustache and mutter Welsh curses, for after fifteen years Eamon de Valera had gotten the policy of External Association Lloyd George had denied him in 1921.

Dev felt it was time to present the new Constitution for Ireland that he had been working on. It was approved in the Dail. Now it must go to the people. He dissolved Dail Eireann and called an election in which they would vote not only for their deputies, but the Constitution itself. And to make sure everyone had a good chance to study it, the document was published on the last day of April 1937; the election would not be held until the first day of July.

Dev would have preferred to see a separate election for the Dail, if that could have been arranged. What if the Constitution were approved, Fianna Fail defeated? The total membership of the Dail was being reduced from 153 to 138. Room could not be found for all former members. In this kind of election, anything could happen.

On the last day of June, Eamon de Valera had some forebodings. But he had always had faith in the people of Ireland. He must continue to trust them now.

"Other people see things and say 'why?' But I dream
things that never were and I say 'why not?' "
George Bernard Shaw

14

THE FIGHT TO
BE NEUTRAL

ON THE MORNING of July 1, 1937, only a small child or a blind
man in Ireland had not read de Valera's Constitution.

"I'm reminded of the 1916 Proclamation," said an old
I.R.A. man in Dublin.

The similarity was marked. As Patrick Pearse had appealed
to all Irishmen "In the Name of God and of the dead generations from which Ireland receives her tradition of nationhood," the Preamble to this new Constitution was written
"In the Name of the Most Holy Trinity" and acknowledged
the heroic and unremitting struggle of Irish heroes for the
rightful independence of their country.

Some questioned the wording of the paragraph which referred to Ireland as a Christian nation.

"What will our Jewish neighbors say to that?" asked one.

His companion laughed. "Did you not hear about Dev's
good friend, Bob Briscoe, when the deputies were arguing
over putting a crucifix in the Dail? Briscoe said if it would

make them better Christians he could see no objection to it!"

Of course those who mourned the passing of British rule in Free Ireland did not like Dev's plan of government, but they were in the minority. The Constitution was approved. And de Valera's party came back with a working majority of 69 in the new Dail. If Labor continued to vote with them, Fianna Fail could continue to govern.

The unanimous choice of all parties for President was Dr. Douglas Hyde, who for fifty years had been teaching Gaelic and crusading for its adoption in all of Ireland. He had never taken sides politically. And his election confirmed the "freedom of conscience and of worship" called for in the new Constitution, for Dr. Hyde was a Protestant. On the morning of his inauguration as Prime Minister, de Valera and the Catholic members of Parliament attended a solemn Votive Mass in St. Mary's Pro-Cathedral, the new President and Protestant deputies worshiped in the Episcopal St. Patrick's Cathedral.

"In you we greet the successor of our rightful princes," said a beaming de Valera after the ceremony of installation in Dublin Castle. And President Hyde received the honors of former princes, for his office took the place of the governor-generalship, and he was installed in the great house in Phoenix Park from which the British Viceroys had ruled.

The Constitution went into effect at the end of December. Shortly after the first of the year, the Prime Minister told the Dail that he was about to go to London to meet representatives of the British Government.

"To discuss Partition?" asked the reporters as he came out of the chamber.

"Inevitably," said de Valera.

For his work in keeping the Six Counties of northeast Ireland within the British Empire, Sir James Craig had been knighted. Using his new title of Lord Craigavon, he promptly announced a general election, to be held while talks between English and Irish delegates were going on in London.

"For all the world," said a morose Derry Nationalist, "like an old bull bawling defiance from a pasture he has appropriated—except it's the tricolor instead of a red rag he's pawing the ground about."

Those in the Six Counties who wished to join the Irish Free State could do little but make wry jests about Craigavon and his government. Every district had been so gerrymandered it was possible only to re-elect their present anti-Irish representatives. But Craigavon hailed the election results as an overwhelming victory and trumpeted his scorn of this "latest demand from southern Ireland for the surrender of Ulster!"

"Lord Craigavon makes a mistake," said de Valera bluntly. "So long as this nation endures, the recovery of that part of the province of Ulster which has been wrongfully torn away, will be the first item on the agenda in *every* conference between the representatives of Ireland and Britain, until that item is finally wiped off in the only way in which it can be wiped off, by the restoration of Ireland's natural unity."

De Valera knew England would continue to back Craigavon's stand. But there were other concessions to be wrung from the British, if enough time remained for negotiations. Hitler's Germany grew more menacing with each passing hour. In mid-February, the Irish talks in London had to be interrupted because England's Prime Minister was busy with affairs in Germany and Austria. And on March 12, Hitler's armies marched into Austria.

"World War II?" said de Valera. "God forbid!"

But the English apparently thought their entrance into the war inevitable and decided they would like to have a friendly Ireland at their back. In April they signed three agreements with the Irish. One transferred back to Ireland the three great ports which the British had occupied since the Treaty. Another saw a payment of ten million pounds by the Irish settle English claims and abolish all penal duties against

goods of both countries. The third provided for trad
ments of mutual advantage. Even Cosgrave's Opp
party in Ireland hailed the "good sense of both sides
the agreements were duly ratified in London and Dub

In Dail Eireann, during discussion of return of the Irish
ports, a startling bit of information was revealed by William
Cosgrave. He testified that in 1928 the British had wanted
Ireland to take over the ports, but he had declined because
of the cost of maintaining them!

De Valera could scarcely believe his ears, but the man who
had been Minister of Defense in 1928 confirmed the statement.

This made some of the Dail suspicious of the present
agreements, and one Labor member inquired whether Dev
had agreed to let the British use the ports as military bases.

"I did not," he said flatly. The Irish were not only going to
hold those ports, they were going to maintain and modernize
them. Ireland must never allow anyone to use her territory
as a base of attack against England.

In December 1938 de Valera was elected President of the
League of Nations Assembly. He was in Geneva when Brit-
ain's Prime Minister, Neville Chamberlain, went to Munich
to negotiate with Hitler. When Dev returned to Ireland the
Opposition party met him with angry protests because of
Ireland's lack of preparedness in case of war. England's Prime
Minister had bought time with his Munich agreement, they
said, but how long would it be before another crisis?

"Dev is still more engrossed with Partition than he is with
the threat of war," said a Fianna Fail deputy, and saw his
belief confirmed in October when de Valera outlined a de-
tailed plan to end Partition, one which would make it as
easy as possible for Belfast and the Six Counties to join Free
Ireland.

But the day after the plan was published, Lord Craigavon
came back with his old battle cry: *No Surrender!*

De Valera felt he must continue his efforts to heal the painful division of his country. Partition was the only problem which remained to prevent friendship between Ireland and England. He was informed—reliably, he believed—that if everyone in Ireland were allowed to vote, the verdict would be four to one for a united nation.

When Partition was put into effect eighteen years before, Lloyd George had warned that the boundary was based "neither on national features or broad geographical considerations," that the majority of Irish would never accept it and the English, in good conscience, would not enforce it. Yet there it was still, straggling up- and downhill, through the middle of houses, between Donegal and Derry, keeping the majority of the people in Fermanagh and Tyrone from joining the free nation they yearned for—it did not make sense. Irish people all over the world were against it. If Dev could just bring to bear the force of public opinion——

He might have brought it off, but the last organization in the world which should have interfered chose that moment to burst, literally, into violence. Irish Republican Army bombs began to explode, and in England! Their aim? To end Partition. Although de Valera denounced them, a wave of anti-Irish sentiment swept through Britain.

And then, with World War II almost upon them, the British announced a military draft. This time there would be no question of conscription in Free Ireland, but what about the Six Counties? What about the Catholic Nationalist third of the population ruled by Lord Craigavon's vaunted Protestant Parliament and Protestant government?

There was a news release on May 1, 1939, from Belfast in which six Catholic Bishops, headed by their Cardinal, issued a statement declaring any attempt to impose conscription in Northern Ireland would be an outrage and an aggression upon their national rights.

Yet on May 3 a London newspaper headlined: LORD CRAIG-

AVON INSISTS ON A POLICY OF MILITARY CONSCRIPTION. The old grizzly was proving just as aggressive as he had been in 1917.

The next day Prime Minister de Valera told the Dail that his government had protested to the English in the strongest possible terms against conscription in the northeast. The whole Dail supported his position.

The British decided against conscripting anyone at all across the Irish Channel. And their Prime Minister assured them that "The people of Northern Ireland are above all loyal to the Crown and to the Connection with the rest of the United Kingdom."

When the British Military Training Bill became law toward the end of May, de Valera antagonized the English further by his claim that Irish citizens living and working in England should be exempt from the draft. Although his claim was denied, the British were extremely lenient when it came to enforcing the bill, exempting all Irish who had lived in England two years or less, and even those who had been there longer, if they could prove they were there temporarily or for purposes of study.

On the last day of August 1939, a visitor was announced in Prime Minister de Valera's office. It was the German minister for Ireland.

"What will be the attitude of your government in the event of a European war?" he asked, coming straight to the point.

De Valera was noncommittal. A few days earlier a German–Soviet nonaggression pact had been published. So had an agreement of mutual assistance between England and Poland.

"If war comes, the Germans will respect Irish neutrality," said the German Minister reassuringly.

De Valera's brown eyes studied him. Then Dev said quietly, "Ireland wishes to be at peace with Germany as well as with other states." The interview was over.

He had few illusions about Germany's respect for anyone's

neutrality. He was not greatly surprised the following day when, without a word of warning, much less a declaration of war, Germany marched into Poland.

But whether he approved of Hitler's actions or not, de Valera felt Ireland must, at all costs, remain neutral. As Dail Eireann considered emergency legislation to deal with the situation, Dev said, "It is only natural that as individual human beings, we should sympathize with one side or another. But I do not think that anyone, no matter what his feelings might be, would suggest that the official policy of this State should be other than what the government will suggest."

He looked at their sober faces, understanding well their resentment toward Germany, feeling they must keep in mind Ireland's peculiar position in the crisis.

"We, of all nations, know what force used by a stronger nation against a weaker one means. We have known what invasion and partition mean. We are not forgetful of our own history. And as long as our own country *or any part of it* is subject to force, the application of force by a stronger nation, it is only natural that our people . . . in looking at their country, consider what its interests should be and what its interests are."

The following day Great Britain and France declared war on Germany. All the member states of the British Commonwealth followed suit. In spite of her quibbling about External Association, Ireland was still considered one of them by the other dominions. When she refused to go into the war, everyone concluded that Germany was going to seize her and use her as a military base.

But Ireland stood stubbornly by her policy, although more than one wise character called it "Neutrality in favor of England!"

So many young volunteers went north across the border to enlist in the British Army that the ratio of men from Free Ireland fighting for England was higher than that from the

Six Counties, which were British territory. British planes forced down in Ireland were quietly repaired, refueled, and sent on their way.

Except for being refused the use of Irish ports, England could not have had a more cooperative neighbor. Yet de Valera insisted that Ireland was maintaining her neutrality. When Hitler protested about the great shipments of food flowing to England across the Irish Channel, Dev replied calmly that Ireland would sell to any country that sent money and ships to carry away the stuff. If German ships could not get through the British blockade, that certainly was not the fault of the Irish!

Except for a few bombs dropped here and there, Ireland escaped any real damage until 1941. But one night de Valera's telephone rang and someone cried, "Belfast is burning— German raid!"

"Order the whole Dublin Fire Brigade north," said Dev. His action might be misinterpreted, but no matter. Those under attack were Irishmen. Ireland would go to their aid.

During the entire war, only a few irreconcilables among the Irish Republican Army tried to take advantage of England's difficulty. Their organization had been outlawed by the Dail. Now more laws were passed to keep them under control. Several Germans who parachuted into Ireland and made contact with the I.R.A. were caught and interned. One of them wrote later that he had been hounded by the "English" Secret Service. But although the Irish Defense Department may have been receiving helpful reports from its British counterpart, it needed no English help within the borders of Ireland. Not only was the Irish force highly organized and efficient, but information continually flowed to it from the people themselves, young and old. They had seen what happened in Belgium, in Holland and Norway and Denmark. All those countries would have been neutral if they could. Germany would treat Ireland the same, should she welcome an invasion and become Germany's desired base for an attack on England.

It was solely the partition of Ireland that kept her from joining Great Britain and her allies in the fight against the Nazis. As long as thousands of their compatriots were kept behind that arbitrary boundary and deprived of a fair representation in their government, as long as England poured millions of pounds across the Irish Channel and used all her influence to preserve that artificial boundary, so long would Ireland hold herself aloof from British wars.

The Irish people continued their wholehearted support of Prime Minister de Valera. In the general election of 1943, Fianna Fail received twice the votes given to the Opposition party.

A year later there was yet another election. Traditionally, every Irish newspaper but Fianna Fail's own was against de Valera. Three Opposition parties fought him claw and fang. But the people of Ireland saw their country at peace. Thanks to Dev's program of self-sufficiency they were not only eating well during the emergency, but still able to send quantities of food to England.

And they were a proud people. They liked de Valera's calm but decisive refusal when the United States and England sent a note *demanding* Ireland's entrance into the war. They remembered what he had said in 1939: "This war will ruin victor and vanquished alike."

The 1944 election gave Eamon de Valera his greatest victory. Fianna Fail 76, *Fine Gael* (Cosgrave's old party with a new name) 30, the four smaller parties a total of 32.

A London newspaper summed it up thus: "The results of the election indicate that de Valera is to the people of Ireland what Churchill is to the people of Britain."

"But they chose for leader a stern sure man
    That looked not back on the waste of story:
    For his country he fought in the battle's van,
    And he won her peace and he won her glory."
    "The Poet Captain"—*Thomas MacDonagh*

15

MAN OF DESTINY

ON THE SEVENTH of May 1945 Germany surrendered, and in Europe World War II was over. Shortly thereafter the great, courageous, stubborn man whose fiery and fearless speeches had put heart in the British people and all freedom-loving people in the world, stood before the microphone to give his Victory Address.

Winston Churchill had never forgiven Ireland for wanting to leave the British Empire. He could never understand why she should want to leave it. He had resented even the grudging concessions made by the 1921 Treaty.

"I'd rather have beaten them to their knees," he had said grimly, "and then given them all they asked for—and more."

That his "defeat" by the Irish had been a bone in his throat all these years was recognized by few, perhaps not even by himself. But this present tremendous victory must have reminded him of that long-ago, small defeat. In his speech, heard throughout the world, he chose to ignore all the help England had received from her neighbor to the west during the last six years. He lambasted de Valera by name, because the "approaches which the southern Irish ports and airfields could so easily have guarded were closed by hostile air-crafts and U-Boats."

Churchill lauded the loyalty and friendship of Northern Ireland. He prided himself that England had nobly restrained herself from laying a violent hand on the rest of Ireland when Eamon de Valera was "frolicking" with the German and Japanese representatives (an overblown reference to courtesy calls Dev had made on the German and Japanese representatives during the war).

Sir Winston's final paragraph should have amused the Irish, for in it he included Ireland with the rest of the nations in the British Commonwealth. But by the time he got to his peroration, his Irish listeners were too furious to catch the error. So this was how the British thanked Ireland for all her help! They listened with small patience for their government to reply.

Eamon de Valera waited for three days before making that reply. By then he had his temper well in hand and he began calmly, "I know the kind of answer I am expected to make. I know the reply I would have given a quarter of a century ago. But I have deliberately decided that is not the reply I shall make tonight."

No matter how unworthy they might consider Mr. Churchill's statement, Dev went on, there had been some excuse for him making it in the first flush of victory—an excuse de Valera himself could not claim in this quieter atmosphere. There were, however, some things it was his duty to say, although he would try to say them as dispassionately as he could.

In certain circumstances, Churchill had said he would have violated Irish neutrality and justified his action by Britain's necessity. That, said Dev, would mean that Britain's necessity could become a moral code and when the necessity was sufficiently great, other peoples' rights would no longer count.

It was, said de Valera, precisely this kind of reasoning that had brought on the disastrous succession of wars. World War I and World War II, and should it be World War III?

A teacher, listening to the broadcast, said later it reminded her of Professor de Valera outlining a mathematical formula to her class at Blackrock as, step by step, he built his argument: If Britain could attack Ireland, no small nation that had adjoined a great power could ever hope to go its way in peace.

Then, after giving Churchill credit for resisting the temptation, Dev got down to cases:

"I would like to put a hypothetical question," he said. "It is a question I have put to many Englishmen . . .

"Suppose Germany had won the war, had invaded and occupied England, and after a long lapse of time and many bitter struggles she was finally brought to acquiesce in admitting England's right to freedom, and let England go, but not the whole of England, all but—let us say—the *six southern counties.*"

As his listeners cheered, Dev went on drawing the parallel, supposing that Germany had singled out those six English counties because they commanded the narrow seas and would enable Germany to maintain the security of her own communications—and holding them would, of course, weaken England as a whole.

Then, said Dev's calm voice (and only the sharpest ear could have caught the tremor in it), then he asked his listeners to imagine that Germany became engaged in a great war that was being fought for the freedom of small nations, and he asked:

"Would Mr. Churchill, as an Englishman who believed that his own nation had as good a right to freedom as any other—not freedom for a part merely, but freedom for the whole—would he, whilst Germany still maintained the partition of his country and occupied six counties of it, would he lead this partitioned England to join with Germany in a crusade? I do not think Mr. Churchill would. Would he think the people of partitioned England an object of shame if they stood neutral in such circumstances? I do not think Mr. Churchill would."

There was more, but it was that simple comparison that stuck in peoples' minds. An American soldier, out of uniform and visiting Dublin for the first time, said thoughtfully, "All the newspapers at home had nothing but bad things to say about Mr. de Valera, but when you hear his side of the story, it's an entirely different thing."

Turning to his host, he asked curiously, "What about this boundary business, anyway? It seems funny in a country as small as this one. . . ."

"It isn't funny," said the Irishman. "No, it isn't funny at all—it's a cursed tragedy and there can be no real friendship between England and us until she stops pouring her millions into Belfast to maintain it."

"But why should England want to maintain it?" asked the young American.

"Pride, perhaps—and a general lack of comprehension among the English people. They're the finest in the world in many ways, but they wear blinders when they look at Ireland. God grant it won't be as de Valera says, that England always wakes up too late."

The difference between the English and Irish was vividly pointed up by de Valera's next official act. It would be difficult to imagine an English leader making a religious pilgrimage, but through the sad, worrisome years of the war, Dev had made an oft-repeated vow that if Ireland were preserved from the horrors of war, when it was over, he would make a public pilgrimage of thanksgiving.

It was to Lough Derg he took himself, north to a small island in a little lake amid the moors and purple-heathered hills of County Donegal, to the most penitential pilgrimage in all Europe, according to those who have made it.

Dev's tall figure stood out above the rest as they alighted from the boat that had brought them across a half mile of water to Station Island. With the rest he took off his shoes and paced barefoot around the great basilica, walked the stony paths to the remains of stone cells where fifteen hundred years before, monks who followed St. Patrick remained to pray—for Ireland, perhaps, as de Valera now was praying.

St. Patrick fasted here for forty days, the legend said, and at the end of that mystic period, God expelled from the island the evil spirits which had infested it. Dev's own prayers thanked God for his mercies, but mingled in them must have been the thought of Ireland riven, for the northeast border of the lake marked the boundary of her lost land, and beyond it her exiled citizens mourned.

It would be the devil's way of hindering a man's devotions to keep reminding him of the map of Ireland he carried in his head—County Tyrone which wished to be with Free Ireland lying a short walk to the east and Fermanagh, whose desire was the same, due south; while free Donegal stretched a gull's flight northeast for more than fifty miles. Sir James Craig had excluded Donegal from his domain when the division was made, lest its freedom-loving Catholics overbalance his small number of English and Scottish Protestants.

But for three days de Valera persevered, eating with thanks his bits of dry bread, drinking his black tea—all the food allowed the pilgrims.

Some thought St. Patrick himself must have been praying with the Irish President, for the day of his return to the world, marked by one of those coincidences that others think so strange and Irish take for granted. For on that same day the party of his erstwhile adversary, Winston Churchill, was voted out of office by an ungrateful electorate.

It was all of a piece, an old Irishwoman said, with the sink-ing of the *Lusitania,* that great ship built in Belfast. For had not her unbelieving builders consigned the Pope to hell on every square foot of her hull? That's no way to build an unsinkable ship, she said, and to stay in office, a statesman will do well not to malign his Irish benefactors.

With no such superstitious thoughts in his head, Eamon de Valera went back to Dublin and plunged into the work of government. His task was complicated by the desperate need of friends in Europe, trying to keep alive as they struggled to rebuild their devastated lives and countries. Ireland sent them food and livestock, clothing, goods, and utensils, glad to share her good fortune with those who had so little. And while all this was going on, de Valera and his Cabinet tried to divest themselves of the extraordinary powers all governments assume in wartime, then to take up again their ambitious social program for their people.

That meant more taxes, and since taxes are no more popular in Ireland than in any other country, Dev's party ran into trouble. The election of 1948 resulted in Fianna Fail still holding a larger number of deputies than any other party in the Dail, but all the rest ganged up on him and suddenly Dev was out of office.

William Cosgrave had retired some time before and John Costello became Ireland's new Prime Minister. It was he who cut the final tie with the six northeastern counties by repealing the External Relations Act. De Valera had always held that as long as that slight connection with the British Crown was maintained, the chances were more likely to achieve an undivided Ireland. It was ironic that it should be Costello, member of the old pro-British-Connection Cosgrave party, Fine Gael, who severed the last thread of the connection.

As if they had been waiting for just such an eventuality, the Labour Government in England introduced and passed a new Ireland Act with a guarantee of Partition, the first ever given by Labour.

To the protesting throng that filled O'Connell Street, de Valera pointed out how Britain was supporting the current movement for the unity of Europe, and called it a fantasy to seek the union of diverse states and nations while at the same time she deliberately tried to strike apart and destroy the integrity of Ireland, one of the oldest nations in the world.

In a voice husky with feeling, he said, "We solemnly pledge ourselves never, not until our last breath, to cease to strive against the unjust partition by which it is intended that this claim for unity and freedom will be forever frustrated." And, in Gaelic: "God forbid!"

He had taken advantage of his freedom from official duties —the first in fifteen years—to travel throughout the world, first to the United States, then on to Australia, India, and a visit to the Vatican. Everywhere he went he spoke of Ireland, and Ireland's one remaining sorrow—"harped on it," grumbled a dour Scotsman from Belfast one day.

Dev had a wonderful visit to Israel with his two sons and Bob Briscoe. He went to England to speak to students, and made a side trip to Lincoln Jail, which he had left so unceremoniously back in 1919. Yet Lincoln Jail, and all the others he had known, would always be with Dev. The long years he had spent in dimly lighted cells, living on inadequate food, abused physically and mentally, had contributed to his present state of near-blindness. His difficulty in seeing had been growing worse for a long time and although he had consulted doctors in the United States, in Switzerland, in Ireland, and elsewhere, nothing had been of lasting benefit.

Shortly after Fianna Fail's return to power, Dev went to a famous Swiss clinic for a series of eye operations. As he lay there completely immobile, his ministers came frequently to consult him, to get his advice on all the important problems Ireland faced in those troubled times. He came back to Dublin with eyesight somewhat improved. The next year he made another pilgrimage, to the shrines of Our Lady of Lourdes, of St. Margaret Mary in Paris, to Fatima in Portugal, and the Basilica of St. Ignatius in Spain.

Sir Winston Churchill was British Prime Minister once again, and that September, de Valera went to London and was entertained by Sir Winston at No. 10 Downing Street. On his return, Dev was met at the Dublin airport by a close Franciscan friend, Father Cormac O'Daly, who said jokingly, "How nice it was of Mr. Churchill to have you there and say all those fine things the papers quoted . . ." but Dev answered grimly, "The English are always very nice, if you aren't asking them for anything."

In the historic church of "Adam and Eve," that same Franciscan sat one night studying when the door opened and de Valera stood there with something in his hands.

"What have you there?" asked Father Cormac.

A smile lighted the grave, long face.

"It's an altar stone from an old church." De Valera eased himself against a long table and set his burden down. "It's from the old home in Bruree, from my grandmother's room. My cousins thought I might like to have it. It belongs here."

So, after its long wandering the blessed stone came once more to an altar in the old Franciscan church, with a plaque nearby telling whence it came, and by whom.

"There was a touching aftermath to this," said Father Cormac, "for one day when the President had been in for Mass and as I took his arm to walk out of the church, a man got up from one of the back pews to swing the door wide for us. Mr. de Valera couldn't see him, and it was a pity, for it was Mr. Cosgrave—what a good chance it would have been for them to shake hands—Mr. Cosgrave's a fine man, you know."

Perhaps it happened elsewhere, for Eamon de Valera has

proved himself a man willing to forgive and forget, no matter how bitterly he may have contested earlier battles.

The 1950s saw his party in and out of power twice, but in 1957 Fianna Fail received the most votes the party had ever gotten and the new Dail opened with Eamon de Valera once again Prime Minister. Perhaps his failing eyesight had much to do with his next decision. Certainly he had the appearance and vigor of a man half his age, but in 1959, near the end of President Sean T. O'Kelley's second and final term, Fianna Fail announced that de Valera was their candidate for the office.

It surprised no one that the Long Fellow won again. On June 25, after his inauguration in Dublin Castle, Sean Lemass, new Prime Minister, said to him:

"For over forty years, in war and in peace, in good and in evil days, you have remained a living symbol of the ideals for which so many generations of our race have striven."

So the de Valeras went to Phoenix Park, where the President's House gleams white against the green lawns and greener trees. As the old Irish chieftains were wont to give their wives the sunniest, most pleasant room in the castle, so Sinead de Valera was ensconced in the southwest corner of the great mansion, a room sun-flooded through windows that reached from floor to ceiling, with her own fire on her own hearth, to keep her company when Dev must be away, and this often happened, for although the Irish presidency is but an honorary position, it requires an enormous amount of time to fulfill all its social obligations.

Sinead de Valera had already made a name for herself as an author, writing stories and plays for children with equal ease in Gaelic or English. Her first book of Irish fairy tales was dedicated to the boys and girls of the United States, for whom she had so much affection. And of all the visitors who would ever come to Ireland and be entertained at the President's House, she would remember most warmly young John

Fitzgerald Kennedy, who in Ireland was welcomed as one of their own, home again.

As the American President was leaving, he came running back down the steps of his plane to lift Sinead de Valera off her feet with a great hug, and kiss her farewell. She spoke of him, after his tragic death that autumn, as she spoke of her young Brian, with fondness and heartbreak, but not as one who is dead. They were only a small distance away, and with the years the distance was growing always less.

No television viewer would ever forget the tall, sorrowing figure of Eamon de Valera as he walked between his sons Eamon and Vivion in the funeral procession of President Kennedy. For in addition to the way the American President had strengthened the wonderful ties of friendship between the United States and Ireland, Dev had felt a personal affection for John Kennedy.

The year following, de Valera was back in Washington, D.C., for a speech to Congress. It was the greatest speech ever made in that chamber, said the Irish-Americans, unashamedly wiping tears of pride and joy from their eyes. And those who watched Eamon de Valera stride up the aisle, heard him speak for thirty minutes with no sign of a note to jog his memory, wondered at his self-assurance and knew that no physical handicap would ever keep this man from anything he proposed to do.

There were things still undone, as his first five years of the Irish presidency passed swiftly into his sixth. The Gaelic he had hoped to hear spoken, along with English, throughout Ireland, was still a subject taught in every school, but spoken fluently by only a few. Yet when Dev wore the red ribbon in his buttonhole that signified that he would be glad to speak Gaelic with others, it seemed that someone was always coming along to have a chat in the beautiful language. Perhaps he was again wishing for too much.

Certainly most of his dreams for Ireland had materialized.

Instead of the twenty-six counties of Free Ireland, wasting away—as Lloyd George had predicted, even planned—they were becoming more self-sufficient every year, burgeoning in industry, the production of electric power, the building of countless homes. No longer did young Irishmen and Irishwomen have to emigrate to find work. There were jobs at home for all who wanted them. The Irish Republic had, not one, but two airlines, and her own radio and television networks. Tourists were flocking to fish in her lakes and rivers, to stay in her fine hotels, ride her fine horses, buy fine Irish products in her shops.

And the year 1965 brought the most heartening development of all. In January few people thought much about it when Sean Lemass, Ireland's Prime Minister, went north to Belfast for a conference. Some Corkmen with long memories grumbled when Belfast's Prime Minister, Terence O'Neill, came down shortly afterward to Dublin, but President de Valera quietly rejoiced over this first parley between Irish heads of state since Partition. For years he had been prophesying something of the kind, saying that, if the English Government would take hands off, the Irish people would be able to work out their destiny in friendship and in peace.

How right Dev had been became clear during the following summer when it was announced that North and South Tourist Boards had united to "sell Ireland as a whole" to the outside world. Visitors to the country found themselves able to go back and forth across the border as freely as they wished. To be sure, the political division remained, and so did British and Irish Customs posts, but the many new roads opened between the two states benefited native Irish as well as tourists. And who could say what further miracles of cooperation might be brought about by the two Tourist Boards, collaborating in their overseas exhibitions and promotional campaigns as if the political border were nonexistent?

This eventful year of 1965, which saw the death in England of Sir Winston Churchill, also saw the remains of Roger Casement brought home, at last, to rest in Irish soil. At the interment, President de Valera spoke movingly of Casement's love for Ulster, ". . . because of the part the people of Ulster had played throughout Ireland's history . . . because he knew that each one of us, next to our own native Province, loves that Province best." And no listener could fail to be stirred by the emotion with which this veteran of the long struggle for Irish freedom begged all who heard him to work for unity with the lost counties, to vie with one another ". . . in loving this land for which so many sacrifices have been made throughout the centuries."

Another few months would see the golden anniversary of the Easter Rising in Dublin. As the willingness of its leaders to die for their country turned defeat into victory, so, perhaps, the willingness of Irish leaders now to work in harmony might turn division into unity, make a resurgent, prosperous Ireland "a nation once again."

Then, indeed, shall ". . . the wild geese spread the grey wing over every tide . . ." when the last great dream of Ireland's Dev, for Ireland, has come true.

GLOSSARY

Article X An article in the League of Nations Agreement which, after World War I, would have preserved the status quo in all possessions of the victorious Allied Powers. The Irish fought it because it seemed likely to keep them forever under British rule. President Wilson's refusal to change so much as a word of it was partially responsible for the refusal of the United States to enter the League of Nations.

Auxiliaries Ex-officers of the British Army, also recruited in England in the spring of 1920, to go to Ireland and assist the police. From a more intelligent class than the Black and Tans, the Auxiliaries were also unruly and held responsible for much of the criminal brutality against the Irish, especially against Irish civilians.

Better Government of Ireland Act, 1920 Known in Ireland as the Partition Act, it provided for two Irish Parliaments, one in Belfast, one in Dublin.

Black and Tans English military forces sent to Ireland in the spring of 1920, dubbed the Black and Tans because of their hastily assembled uniforms: khaki coats, black trousers and caps.

Blue Shirts Originally a civil, unarmed organization pledged to "give disciplined service to the nation," the members, in 1933, adopted the uniform of a blue shirt. The following year some of the Blue Shirts got out of control and encouraged farmers to refuse to pay their taxes, cut telephone wires, felled trees to block roads, impeding officials who attempted to collect taxes.

Boundary Commission Set up in Clause 12 of the 1921 Treaty, the commission was supposed to determine "in accordance with the wishes of the inhabitants," the boundaries between the northeast and the rest of Ireland.

British Ascendancy Descendants of English and Scotsmen who had taken possession of Irish land through the centuries of British rule. Protestant and pro-British, they maintain absolute political control of the six northeastern counties of Ireland.

Clause 12 of the 1921 Treaty The clause which provided for a commission to determine the boundary between northeastern Ireland and the Irish Free State.

Coalition Government Provided for in the Collins-de Valera Pact of 1922, this was to be a government in which the pro-Treaty party and anti-Treaty Republicans were to keep their respective strengths until tempers had time to cool and agreements could be worked out in regard to the Treaty with the British. The British insisted on scrapping the pact and civil war followed.

Dail Eireann The Irish Parliament.

Dublin Brigade Irish Republican Army forces in Dublin whose special Active Service Unit engaged in street-fighting, ambushing British patrols and destroying enemy transport during the war against England.

External Association A compromise policy by which de Valera hoped to bring the northeastern counties into an all-Ireland Parliament, this would have brought Ireland, recognizing the British Crown as an independent nation, into free association with the British Commonwealth.

Fianna Eireann An organization for boys under sixteen, this preparatory course for the Irish Volunteers was directed by the Countess Markievicz before the Rising. The boys carried messages, made bombs, learned to shoot, and dedicated themselves to the ideal of Irish independence.

Fianna Fail A Gaelic phrase meaning "Army of Destiny," this was the political party formed by Eamon de Valera in April 1926 after he resigned from Sinn Fein.

Fine Gael Gaelic name for the political party which opposed Fianna Fail.

Gaelic and Gaelic League Gaelic was the language spoken by the

Irish people; it is also referred to as the Irish language. The Gaelic League was a cultural society, formed in 1893, whose aim was the preservation of Gaelic as a spoken tongue.

Home Rule Self-government for the Irish people. As the measure was originally introduced, it provided for a certain measure of British control.

Irish Convention A convention of Irishmen called by Lloyd George in 1917, ostensibly to formulate proposals for the future government of Ireland within the British Empire, actually "to keep the Irish talking, while England persuaded the United States to come into World War I."

Irish Free State Name given to the twenty-six counties of Ireland whose representatives had signed the 1921 Treaty with the British.

Irish Parliamentary party Irish Representatives who sat in the British Parliament after the Act of Union, 1800.

Irish Republic The Independent self-government desired by most Irish Nationalists before 1921.

Irish Republican Army, or I.R.A. The name applied to the official Irish Army after 1920, formerly called the Irish Volunteers. After establishment of the Irish Free State, the I.R.A. split. In later years the name was applied to the rebellious faction continually stirring up trouble against the government.

Irish Republican Brotherhood, or the I.R.B. A secret political organization dating from 1858, pledged to establish an Irish Republic by force.

Irish Volunteers The Irish Army was organized in November 1913 under the leadership of Professor Eoin MacNeill at the instigation of the I.R.A., whose aim was to secure and maintain the rights and liberties common to all the people of Ireland without distinction of creed, class or politics. At the outbreak of World War I most of the Volunteers joined the British Army. Those who did not were the fighting men who distinguished themselves in the 1916 Rising against the British.

Labor's Citizen Army Made up of members of the Transport and General Workers Union who began drilling in military formation late in 1913 during the great Dublin strike. With James Connolly at their head, about a hundred of them fought in the Easter Rising.

Land League An organization of Irish peasants, founded by Michael Davitt in 1879, whose aim was to obtain for those who worked the land fair rent, fixed tenure and the right of free sale, and eventually to restore the ownership of Irish land to the Irish who worked it.

Oath of Allegiance The oath swearing allegiance to the British Crown, required by the Anglo-Irish Treaty of 1921.

"Orange" Forces A militantly anti-Catholic and pro-British organization in northeastern Ireland, founded in 1795 to maintain a Protestant Ascendancy, and used after 1886 as a political tool by English Tories in an attempt to defeat Home Rule for Ireland and stir up religious antagonism between Catholic and Protestant.

Partition The arbitrary division of Ireland accomplished by the British Parliament in 1920 under the leadership of Prime Minister Lloyd George.

Penal Days The period following the breaking of the Treaty of Limerick by the English, during which statutes were enacted to hold the Irish in a condition of servitude, especially the Catholic and Presbyterian Irish.

Public Safety Acts This phrase usually refers to measures taken by the Free State Government in 1923–24 by which persons might be imprisoned without trial.

1798 Rebellion An Irish insurrection against the British led by two Protestant Irishmen, Wolfe Tone and Lord Edward Fitzgerald.

The Rising, or the Easter Rising The Irish insurrection, mainly in Dublin, on Easter Monday 1916, whose aim was to throw off British rule and establish self-government for Ireland.

Royal Irish Constabulary, or R.I.C. An auxiliary police force recruited among Irishmen, commanded by the British and established in fortified posts all over the country, highly respected until the Irish rebellion of 1916–21, during which it gradually deteriorated.

Sinn Fein A Gaelic phrase meaning "Ourselves Alone," chosen in 1905 by Arthur Griffith to apply to those who believed that the best way to achieve Irish emancipation was through passive resistance, abstention from the British Parliament and concentration on national aims. Mistakenly applied to leaders of the 1916 Rising, Sinn Fein later became the title for the party of Nationalist Ireland.

The Six Counties Derry, Antrim, Down, Armagh, Trone and Fermanagh, the counties in Ireland still under British rule.

Statute of Westminster A statute resulting from the recommendations by six member States of the British Commonwealth (Canada, Australia, New Zealand, South Africa, the Irish Free State and Newfoundland) insisting on their equality with England. Approved by the British Parliament, it received the Royal Assent in 1931.

Treaty of Limerick An Anglo-Irish Treaty signed in 1691 by the great Irish hero and soldier Patrick Sarsfield and King William, it was to give Catholics of Ireland the same privileges they had enjoyed under Charles II. It was after breaking of this Treaty that the Penal Days began.

Ulster An ancient Irish kingdom which became one of Ireland's four great Provinces and now contains nine counties. Ulster is often—erroneously—applied to the six northeastern counties in Ireland still under British rule.

Ulster "Specials" A special Protestant police force in northeast Ireland armed as soldiers and stationed in every village and town. Founded in 1920 to maintain the British Ascendancy and fight Irish Home Rule, in 1955–56 they numbered over 11,000 (although the regular police force numbered only 3,000) and at that strength police the Six Counties more heavily than any others in Ireland.

Unionists Those in Ireland who preferred to remain under British rule.

White Cross Fund Money and supplies collected by the American Committee for Relief in Ireland during the Irish war for independence. Each state in the Union assumed responsibility for one devastated area in Ireland. Funds were also collected in England, Canada and Scotland.

SELECTED BIBLIOGRAPHY

The whole picture—a few Irish histories:

Carty, James. *Ireland*. Dublin: C. J. Fallon, 1957–58

Curtayne, Alice. *The Irish Story*. Dublin: Clonmore & Reynolds, 1962

Inglis, Brian. *The Story of Ireland*. London: Faber & Faber, 1956.

Landreth, Helen, *Dear Dark Head*. New York: Whittlesey House, 1936

MacArdle, Dorothy. *The Irish Republic*. London: Gollancz, 1937; Dublin: Irish Press, 1951

O'Hegarty, P. S. *A History of Ireland Under the Union*. Dublin: Talbot, 1922

O'Sullivan, Donal. *The Irish Free State and Its Senate*. London: Faber & Faber, 1940

Trevelyan, G. M. *History of England*. New York: Doubleday Anchor, 1952

Woodham-Smith, Cecil. *The Great Hunger*. New York: Harper, 1962

Other biographies of Eamon de Valera:

Bromage, Mary C. *De Valera*. London: Hutchinson, 1956

Douglas, James G. *President de Valera and the Senate*. Dublin: Eason, 1934

MacManus, M. J. *Eamon de Valera*. Dublin: Talbot, 1944–62

O'Doherty, Katherine. *Assignment: America*. New York: de Tanko, 1957

O'Faolain, Sean. *De Valera*. Harmondsworth, Middlesex: Penguin, 1939

Biographies of other Irish patriots (plus a good bit of history):
Beaslai, Piaras. *Michael Collins.* Dublin: Phoenix, 1926
Briscoe, Robert. *For the Life of Me.* Boston: Little, Brown, 1958
Colum, Padraic. *Arthur Griffith.* Dublin: Browne & Nolan, 1959
Landreth, Helen. *The Pursuit of Robert Emmett.* New York: Whittlesey House, 1948
Lavelle, Patricia O'Mara. *James O'Mara.* Dublin: Clonmore & Reynolds, 1961
Le Roux, Louis N. *Patrick H. Pearse.* Dublin: Talbot, 1932
MacBride, Maud Gonne. *A Servant of the Queen.* Dublin: Standard, 1950
O'Brien, Conor C. *Parnell and His Party.* Oxford: Oxford University Press, 1957
O'Brien, Nora Connolly. *Portrait of a Rebel Father.* Dublin: Talbot, 1935
O'Connor, Frank. *The Big Fellow.* London, New York: Nelson, 1937
O'Faolain, Sean. *Constance Markievicz.* London: Cape, 1934
O'Hegarty, P. S. *A Short Memoir of Terence MacSwiney.* Dublin: Talbot, 1922
———. *The Victory of Sinn Fein.* Dublin: Talbot, 1924
Parmiter, G. de C. *Roger Casement.* London: Barker, 1936
Taylor, Rex. *Assassination.* London: Hutchinson, 1961

Biographies and recollections connected with Ireland:
Birkenhead, 2nd Earl of. *The Last Phase,* by his Son, London: Butterworth, 1935
Churchill, Winston. *The Aftermath.* London: Butterworth, 1929
———. *Thoughts and Adventures.* London: Macmillan, 1942
Crozier, Frank P. *Ireland Forever!* London: Cape, 1932
Macready, Sir Nevil. *Annals of an Active Life.* London: Hutchinson, 1924
Pakenham, Frank. *Peace by Ordeal.* London: Chapman & Hall, 1962
Shakespeare, Sir Geoffrey. *Let Candles Be Brought In.* London: Macdonald, 1949
Smith, Gene. *When the Cheering Stopped.* New York: Morrow, 1964

The Rising and the Troubles:
Bennett, Richard. *The Black and Tans.* Boston: Houghton Mifflin, 1960
Caulfield, Max. *The Easter Rebellion.* New York: Holt, Rinehart and Winston, 1963

Collins, Michael. *The Path to Freedom*. Dublin: Talbot, 1922
Colum, Padraic. *Ourselves Alone!* New York: Crown, 1959
Gleeson, James. *Bloody Sunday*. London: Davies, 1962
Ryan, Desmond. *The Rising*. Dublin: Golden Eagle, 1949

Ireland and the Irish from literary points of view:
Brennan, Robert Edward. *Irish Diary*. Westminster, Md.: Newman, 1962
Carbery, Mary. *Happy World*. London, New York: Longmans, 1941
Colum, Padraic. *The Road Round Ireland*. New York: Macmillan, 1926
————. *Anthology of Irish Verse*. New York: Liveright, 1948
de Valera, Sinead. *The Emerald Ring and Other Fairy Tales*. New York: Dodd, Mead, 1951
Edgeworth, Maria. *Castle Rackrent*. London, New York: Oxford, 1964 (new ed.)
Frankenberg, Lloyd (ed.). *A James Stephens Reader*. New York: Macmillan, 1962
Gibbings, Robert. *Lovely Is the Lee*. New York: Dutton, 1945
Hanna, D. O'D. *The Face of Ulster*. London, New York: Batsford, 1952
Hoagland, Kathleen. *1000 Years of Irish Poetry*. New York: Devin-Adair, 1947
Inglis, Brian. *West Briton*. London: Faber & Faber, 1962
O'Casey, Sean. *Inishfallen Fare Thee Well*. New York: Macmillan, 1949
————. *Drums Under the Windows*. New York: Macmillan, 1960 (paper)
O'Connor, Frank. *An Only Child*. New York: Knopf, 1961
O'Faolain, Sean. *An Irish Journey*. London: Longmans, 1940
————. *Vive Moi!* Boston: Little, Brown, 1963
O'Flaherty, Liam. *The Informer*. London: Cape, 1949
————. *Insurrection*. London: Gollancz, 1950
Robinson, Lennox. *A Golden Treasury of Irish Verse*. New York: Macmillan, 1925

Books, old and new, about Ireland:
Armour, W. S. *Facing the Irish Question*. London: Duckworth, 1935
Callan, Luke B. *Ireland After Forty Years*. Boston: Angel Guardian, 1933
Duff, C. *Ireland and the Irish*. New York: Boardman, 1952

Falls, C. B. *The Birth of Ulster*. London: Methuen, 1936
Green, A. S. A. *Ourselves Alone in Ulster*. Dublin: Maunsel, n.d.
Harbinson, R. *No Surrender*. London: Faber & Faber, 1960
Harrison, Henry. *Ulster and the British Empire*. London: R. Hale, 1939
———. *The Neutrality of Ireland, Why It Was Inevitable*. London: R. Hale, 1942
Jackson, T. A. *Ireland Her Own*. New York: International, 1947
Kelly, R. S. *Ireland's Bloodless Revolution*. Chicago: Joyce & Smith, 1936
Lepper, J. H. *Famous Secret Societies*. London: Low, Marston, 1932
Leslie, Shane. *The Irish Tangle*. London: Macdonald, 1946
Mansergh, Nicholas. *Britain and Ireland*. London, New York: Longmans, 1942
Maxwell, Constantia E. *The Stranger in Ireland*. London: Cape, 1954
Meenan, J. F. *A View of Ireland*. Dublin: British Association for the Advancement of Science, 1957
Molony, J. C. *The Riddle of the Irish*. London: Methuen, 1927
O'Hegarty, P. S. *Ulster*. Dublin: Maunsel, 1919
Sheed, F. J. *The Irish Way*. New York: Kenedy, 1932

Special recommendations:
Gallagher, Frank. *The Indivisible Island*. London: Gollancz, 1957. About the Partition of Ireland.
Kennedy, P. G., S.J. *An Irish Sanctuary*. London: Hutchinson, 1956. For the birdwatcher.
Killanin, Lord, and Michael V. Duignan. *Illustrated Guide to the Counties of Ireland* (Irish Tourist Board, Dublin Shell Guide to Ireland). New York: Norton, 1962. For the history and antiquities enthusiast.
O'Callaghan, Sean. *The Jackboot in Ireland*. London: Wingate, 1958. Germany's subversion attempts in Ireland, World War II.

Speeches and a pamphlet by Eamon de Valera:
Peace and War: Speeches 1932–38. Dublin: Gill, 1944
"The Unity of Ireland." Dublin: Stationery Office, 1939

INDEX

E12

Manhasset Public Library
Manhasset, New York

Hours
Monday through Saturday
9:00-5:30
Monday, Wednesday, Friday Eves.
7:00-9:00

The borrower is responsible for all
books and other materials drawn on
his card.

DO NOT REMOVE DATE CARD FROM POCKET